# PRAISE FOR *THE 1-MINUTE WRITER*

"Creative writing forces us to engage our imagin[ation] and spirit of invention. But it's also a discipline: [we must set aside] time, push aside distractions, and trust that our brains are up to a ch[allenge]. In a breezy, encouraging, utterly approachable style, Leigh Medeiros eases your mind into creativity with fun and thought-provoking exercises, each meant to help you with writing's most difficult step: starting."

—Stephen Thompson, editor and reviewer for NPR Music

"If I'd had *The 1-Minute Writer* when I'd started out, I bet there'd be a lot more words in my books!"

—James Yang, author and illustrator of *The New York Times* Standout New Picture Book *Bus! Stop!*

"The author's prompts feel more like play than practice. They are joyful, creative, and approachable. Medeiros brings her infectious positive energy and encouragement—which I've had the pleasure of experiencing in her 48 Days of Creative Devotion program—to *The 1-Minute Writer*. It's a road map to a daily writing practice, a remedy for bouts of writer's block, and a delightful way to build and stretch those writing muscles. I can't wait to share this book with students in my writing workshops."

—Anika Denise, author of *Lights, Camera, Carmen!* and *Planting Stories: The Life of Librarian and Storyteller Pura Belpré*

"One of the most significant takeaways from my years of helping children unleash their inner playwrights is the notion that our innate ability to write is just below the surface—all that we need is to be provided with triggers that nurture that ability. The thoughtfully crafted and utterly accessible prompts found in the excellent *The 1-Minute Writer*, whether inspired by the everyday around us, gleaned from our wiliest imaginations, or harvested from our own personal histories, do just that—and help unleash our own omnipresent inner writers."

—Jenny Peek, founder and former executive artistic director of The Manton Avenue Project

# PRAISE FOR *THE 1-MINUTE WRITER*

"It's difficult to do anything from a dead start. You need momentum, something you can build from, and that's precisely what this book provides: a creative wind in your sail."

—Chris Sparling, screenwriter of *Buried* and *The Sea of Trees*

"At last! A gift to educators everywhere—a book that supports teachers in all disciplines to integrate writing as an everyday practice. Organized by theme and cataloged by number of minutes, this delightful and accessible text is essential for all classroom teachers. Medeiros provides a plethora of prompts that fuel the imagination while establishing important writing structures. Planning for writing made easy and enjoyable!"

—Uzma Hossain, educational consultant at
Teachers College, Columbia University

"Somehow Leigh Medeiros manages to pull off a seemingly impossible paradoxical feat with this must-have book: she manages to get us out of our brains and into our imaginations. This book is like a Choose Your Own Adventure for grownups who want to write their own endings—396 of them to be exact! These prompts are a godsend for anyone who loves words: playful, ingenious flints that will surely spark even the most hesitant writer to fiery prose. Hot metaphors aside, if you're anything like me and find yourself creating more excuses not to write than creating actual sentences you're proud of, I guarantee this book will leave you feeling warm, inspired, and—most remarkably—accomplished. No longer will we look at time spent standing in a checkout line or riding a bus as "wasted"; you will relish every opportunity to dive into another thoughtful prompt. I only wish *The 1-Minute Writer* had been around decades ago to vanquish my inner procrastinator and catalyze my creative impulses. I can't wait to pull this book of clever what-ifs off the shelf for many years to come, whenever the well of creativity runs dry or the rust on my wrist sets in."

—Paul Walling, actor and writer

# The
# 1-MINUTE
# Writer

**396 Microprompts to Spark
Creativity and Recharge Your Writing**

Leigh Medeiros

Adams Media
New York    London    Toronto    Sydney    New Delhi

To teachers like Carlton Pinheiro who nurture
creative thinking and to parents like mine who
never stifle outlandish dreams.

**A** **adams**media

Adams Media
An Imprint of Simon & Schuster, Inc.
57 Littlefield Street
Avon, Massachusetts 02322

First Adams Media trade paperback edition January 2019

ADAMS MEDIA and colophon are trademarks of Simon & Schuster.

For information about special discounts for bulk purchases, please contact Simon & Schuster Special Sales at 1-866-506-1949 or business@simonandschuster.com.

The Simon & Schuster Speakers Bureau can bring authors to your live event. For more information or to book an event contact the Simon & Schuster Speakers Bureau at 1-866-248-3049 or visit our website at www.simonspeakers.com.

Interior design by Katrina Machado

Manufactured in the United States of America

10  9  8  7  6  5  4  3  2  1

Library of Congress Cataloging-in-Publication Data
Names: Medeiros, Leigh, author.
Title: The 1-Minute writer / Leigh Medeiros.
Description: Avon, Massachusetts: Adams Media, 2019.
Identifiers: LCCN 2018033587 | ISBN 9781507209288 (pb) | ISBN 9781507209295 (ebook)
Subjects: LCSH: English language–Composition and exercises. | English language–Rhetoric–Problems, exercises, etc. | Creative writing. | BISAC: REFERENCE / Writing Skills. | LANGUAGE ARTS & DISCIPLINES / Composition & Creative Writing. | SELF-HELP / Creativity.
Classification: LCC PE1413 .M43 2019 | DDC 808/.042–dc23
LC record available at https://lccn.loc.gov/2018033587

ISBN 978-1-5072-0928-8
ISBN 978-1-5072-0929-5 (ebook)

# CONTENTS

# ACKNOWLEDGMENTS

Deep and sincere thanks to everyone who helped bring this book to light. To my acquisitions editor Cate Prato for nurturing my writing and enthusiastically shepherding this project through all its various stages. To my developmental editor Brett Shanahan for making the work better with her keen eye and attention to detail. To all the Adams Media team for their support of me and this book. To my fellow writers and visual artists in my online community who inspire me to continue showing up for creativity. To my husband Mark for loving me through all of my quirks and for picking up the slack on deadline weeks. To Emily, Sarah, Janice, Jill, Jo, Jen, Andre, Eric and all the other friends and family who sent encouraging messages, texts, and emails as the book was being born. To Kate and Anika for not only being accomplished authors who inspire me, but also for being ones I can turn to for a writer's perspective on the book-birthing process. To Ada and Bob, my parents, for a lifetime of support, without which I wouldn't have the courage to follow all my creative whims. To my local coffee shops and public library for providing warm atmospheres and de facto office space throughout the writing journey. To the makers of the Coffitivity and Self Control apps for helping writers like me to focus. To the benevolent, mysterious, invisible forces of the universe that work behind the scenes and help guide my decisions so that everything lines up at the perfect time. Finally, to all the writers and readers who came before and will come after, because words connect us through time and space—and connection is key.

# INTRODUCTION

So often people carry the false belief that creative writing requires hours of uninterrupted time clacking away inside a bubble far from the distractions of the world. The reality is that writing for just 1 minute each day will strengthen your creative muscles more than writing for 20 minutes every two weeks—and minutes are a lot easier to come by than hours. After all, creative potential doesn't just exist within large swaths of unhurried time, but in life's in-between moments too. Moments like standing by the front door waiting for your work carpool to arrive or zoning out in the dentist's office while your kiddos get their teeth cleaned. These typically unmemorable microperiods of time are available for your creative benefit. With the help of *The 1-Minute Writer*, you can reclaim them and painlessly bring writing into your day-to-day life.

Each of the prompts in this book contains an unfinished idea that—with the striking of a conceptual match (i.e., putting pen to page or fingers to keyboard)—can spark your creativity. They can help you break through whatever obstacle is in the way of your writing, whether it's exhaustion or a nasty creative block. They're also just a whole lot of fun. You can use these prompts to keep your writing muscles flexed or you can use them to kick-start new projects.

Whichever way you work with these prompts, do so with an eager sense of discovery. Your creative potential is vast, and it lies in wait like a field of dormant seeds. The only thing needed to stimulate that growth is a single spare minute.

# HOW THIS BOOK WORKS

You'll find ninety-nine prompt themes in this book, each one comprised of four timed prompts: 1 minute, 5 minutes, 10 minutes, and 20 minutes. When using the 1-minute prompts you'll be able to get down two to three cleverly crafted sentences. With the 5 and 10-minute prompts you can spend more time with the concept of the prompt theme, resulting in one paragraph to several paragraphs of wild musings. The 20-minute prompts are slightly more complex than the others and are designed to be more of a deep dive. Even if you pause to think for a few moments along the way, you're still likely to end up with a solid page of writing when using these. Of course more important than word count or page count is the sense of heartwarming accomplishment and spine-tingling satisfaction that comes with doing any amount of creative work. Am I right? (Insert you nodding your head here.)

Since everyone's creative impetus is unique, I've separated the ninety-nine prompt themes into three sections: Observation, Imagination, and Memory. Each of these sections has thirty-three prompt themes that offer up different starting points to spark your creativity. The Observation Prompts call on you to observe what's around you and what's within you. The Imagination Prompts rely purely on your mind to conjure a variety of scenarios. The Memory Prompts help you recall past events, interactions, and experiences to mine for creative possibility. All of the sections have prompts that may appeal to both fiction and nonfiction writers of every kind. Some prompts might task you with writing a breaking news report, while others nudge you to come up with lyrics for a silly children's song. Of course feel free to mix and match. If a prompt calls on you to write a eulogy, but you'd rather frame it as a college admissions acceptance letter, go for it. Once you pry it open, your creative mind is truly limitless. If it leads you down a different path than the prompt seems to suggest, follow it with abandon.

An obvious way to choose prompts is to consider the time you have available. Certain days you may have only a few minutes to write, while other days you have half an hour. In that regard you can pick whatever prompt or prompts fit your schedule. Another option, particularly if you're a beginner writer or lapsed writer, is to do all of the 1-minute prompts first, then work your way up incrementally from there. Last, if you want to use the prompts as a starting point for a larger or longer creative work, you may find added benefit in consecutively completing all four prompts in a theme in order to explore an idea from multiple angles.

If you're serious about kick-starting or maintaining a writing practice you should keep this book nearby throughout the day to take full advantage of the spare moments that arise. If carrying the book is too cumbersome or not an option, you can take photographs of various pages with your smartphone then refer to them later. In terms of the actual writing there are several apps you can get for your phone that will allow you to physically type or use voice dictation. These are especially helpful if you're on the go and have only a short period of time to work. Of course you could also opt for the classic bound journal or pocket notepad to handwrite the exercises.

Whatever modes or methods you choose, make sure they easily fit into your lifestyle. The intention is that you can do these prompts anywhere. Break them out while you're standing in line at the bank, as you're waiting for the pasta water to boil, or during your ride to work on the Number 58 bus. The short increments of time involved, especially the 1-minute prompts, will truly eliminate the all too familiar "I don't have time to write" excuse while also giving you a sustainable way to build creative muscle.

Practically speaking, when it comes to timing the prompts keep it as simple as possible. If there's a clock on the office wall or on your car dashboard, use it. If you have a smartphone, pull up the timer application. Not only will it give you an accurate countdown, it will also chime aloud when complete. (Pavlov would certainly approve.) You can also purchase a kitchen timer for less than $10. If at any point all of that feels like too much to handle, just guesstimate the time in your mind. Do what works. Don't overthink it.

Last, my intention has been to make these prompts as inclusive and universal as possible, even while not knowing the specific circumstances of readers. For any prompts that don't quite work for you, for whatever reason, I humbly request that you use your awesome creative power to adjust them as you see fit.

# TIPS FOR GETTING YOUR
# DAILY WRITING ON

This fact is undeniable: creating a daily practice requires commitment. If you're the type of person that feels safe and secure within the confines of commitment, awesome. You've got a leg up. If you're like me—someone who often feels that commitment is like, oh, a death grip squeezing the life out of poor, sorry freedom—then you've got some extra work to do. For folks like us, I include these tips. You may have heard some of them before, but that's only because they always bear repeating.

- Create two goals—a reasonable minimum goal and an ideal goal for your daily and/or weekly writing. Perhaps your minimum goal is 1 hour of writing per week, but your ideal goal is 2 hours. Aim for the 2 hours, but if you fall short you've most likely reached your minimum. The idea is to strive for your ideal but know that achieving your minimum is a worthy accomplishment too.

- Set an umbrella goal based on a predetermined number of days, such as ten days of writing in a row. Umbrella goals provide a container that gives you structure and helps you to move forward. Telling yourself to "write every day" can often be a setup for failure since it's such a large, open-ended goal. I recommend choosing an umbrella goal that feels like a little bit of a stretch, then—when you achieve that goal—set a slightly more ambitious one.

- Find ways to hold yourself accountable to the work. I can't sing the praises of outside accountability enough. You might post daily progress to followers on a social media site, or, perhaps, read your favorite sentence of the day to your partner, child, or friend every evening. Build accountability into your writing practice and you'll be far more likely to stick with it.

- Track your progress with a visual calendar, whether it's on your phone or physically pinned to the fridge. Mark off the days that you write. Seeing what you've accomplished along the way helps motivate you to continue.

- Try devotion instead of discipline. Discipline is often associated with the concept of punishment; devotion is more often used in connection with love. Cultivate devotion in your creative work and you'll be focused on the love of daily practice, not the pain of it.

- Let the writing wander. Follow where it leads you. Release the idea that you're doing anything wrong by straying from your original intent. Trust that the writing has its own wisdom.

- Keep the inner editor at bay while you're using the prompts. Unless there is a horribly misspelled word that might baffle you later, there's no need to revise the text as you go. Even punctuation and grammar can wait.

# OBSERVATION PROMPTS

Observation Prompts call on you to be aware of your internal and external environments. They task you with looking at what's inside of you and what's outside of you. Though every prompt in this book taps into your creative imagination, the Observation Prompts offer a more concrete starting point, and they can be done no matter where you are, whether it's sitting on the couch at home, riding the subway to visit friends, or eating in the school cafeteria. No matter your location, there is always something within you and around you worth exploring in previously unimagined ways. Your external environment is rich with information, from the colors, shapes, and sizes of architectural details, to the earth's natural flora and fauna, to an abundance of manufactured objects. Your internal environment is equally as rich. Thoughts, feelings, sensations, and movements are all part of the mix when it comes to observing yourself. Many of the prompts in this section ask you to locate objects nearby; others call on you to focus on a sound; and a few others may require a small action such as getting to a window or feeling something with your hands. The beauty of the Observation Prompts is that they can be used again and again as you find yourself in new environments.

# Sense-ational

## 1-MINUTE PROMPT:

You're on the phone with a far-flung friend who wants to hear about where you are right now. Check out your surroundings. Capture the essence of what you see around you in just a few sentences.

## 5-MINUTE PROMPT:

Have you ever had a literal bad taste in your mouth? Find something nearby that's inedible. Imagine what it would be like to give it a big, slurpy lick. How do you think it might taste? Write a product review for a food website about a newly released item that shares this flavor profile.

# 10-MINUTE PROMPT:

Your experimental musician friend, Lars, likes to find and record interesting sounds. Imagine what you could bang together, step on, throw, or otherwise interact with in your environment to create unique sounds. Write about your collaborative audio experiment with Lars; include details about the sound samples you collect.

# 20-MINUTE PROMPT:

In some not-so-distant future, humans have evolved their sense of smell to match the complexity of a dog's. Take stock of the possible smells in your current environment, from the pleasant (like flowers) to the unpleasant (like rotting garbage). Imagine future law enforcement agents moving through your space on the scented trail of a suspect. What do they smell and how does it help or hinder their investigation?

# State of the Union

 ## 1-MINUTE PROMPT:

Close your eyes and check in with your body. Start with the top of your head and scan down to your toes. Check for places where you're holding tension. What's your posture or pose like? Where are your muscles relaxed or contracted? Write about your current state.

 ## 5-MINUTE PROMPT:

You're an extraterrestrial who's been dropped into the human body you now inhabit. Wiggle around a little bit. Flex and stretch. Looking at your body from the point of view of an outsider, compose a letter to your alien family back home telling them how you're getting along in this new "suit."

# 10-MINUTE PROMPT:

Your body has its own terrain, and you can map it like a cartographer. Check in with it now. Where can you still feel an old wound? Where can you feel a lightness of being? What is the quality of your skin? How open is your heart? Imagine your body as a map that holds many unique areas of interest, from the spot on your face where a loved one kissed you, to that dry patch of skin that never goes away. Write about the actual and symbolic topography of this familiar terrain.

# 20-MINUTE PROMPT:

You've been asked to give a "State of the Union" speech about your body at a doctor's conference. Notice where you feel aches, pains, injuries, or illness. Talk about what policies, procedures, and/or practices you might put in place in the coming year. Think about how your appearance may have changed too. If there's enough time, include reactions to your speech and questions from the crowd.

# Can You Dig It?

## 1-MINUTE PROMPT:

You're tasked with putting together an archaeological dig. Look around; what would be the best spot to excavate archaeological remains? Speculate on what might be found there, whether it's old gum stuck to the pavement or arrowheads along the river bank.

## 5-MINUTE PROMPT:

What's it like to see with new eyes? Find a man-made object nearby. Imagine you've just unearthed it in an archaeological dig and it's the first time you've ever seen it. Write about the moment of discovery, how it feels to pull this object out of the earth and hold it in your hands.

# 10-MINUTE PROMPT:

Pick out two seemingly unrelated objects in your current environment. Imagine that you and another archaeologist have each extracted these objects from your dig site and it's the first time either of you has ever seen them. Describe these objects at length as you discuss the strange discoveries with your colleague.

# 20-MINUTE PROMPT:

Take two unrelated objects that are near you and imagine they're from a culture that's now extinct. Write a scene where you're in a museum looking at these objects encased in glass when, suddenly, the room disappears, and you find yourself hundreds or thousands of years in the past. Finish the scene where you curiously observe people from that culture using these two items.

# Writing Sample

**5-MINUTE PROMPT:** What's it like to see with new eyes? Find a man-made object nearby. Imagine you've just unearthed it in an archaeological dig and it's the first time you've ever seen it. Write about the moment of discovery, how it feels to pull this object out of the earth and hold it in your hands.

## SAMPLE:

With one last tug I pull the object from the earth. Gently, I take a brush to its surface, releasing centuries of dirt and debris. For the first time I'm able to get a good look at what I've been digging for. It's oblong in shape and half a foot in length. The object, which appears to be a vessel, tapers off to a 1-inch neck where there's a small, round opening. The material is extremely light, like a pile of feathers, and seems to be some kind of polymer. Remarkably, I can see right through it. Inside, there are tiny droplets of a clear liquid. It occurs to me that this could be what the ancestors called "water," but since we haven't had water on Earth for more than three hundred years I push the idea out of my mind. Instead I peer into the tiny opening at the top of the vessel and marvel at how perfectly round it is. I notice, for the first time, a small ring encircling the lip of this tapered neck. With my finger I move it back and forth, then spin it around.

# In and Out

## 1-MINUTE PROMPT:

*Ah, oxygen!* Close your eyes. Take a long, slow, deep breath through your nose. Write a tiny poem about the experience of inhalation without using the word *air*.

## 5-MINUTE PROMPT:

Hold your breath for as long as you can. Feel the pressure build, the rising panic, and how your body aches to breathe. Write about the sensations and thoughts you experienced from the point of view of a character who's underwater.

# 10-MINUTE PROMPT:

Breathe in. Breathe out. Using both fact and nonsense make a list of all the things you can do with your breath right now (e.g., blowing crumbs off the table, cleaning your eyeglasses, and so on). When finished, turn the actions on your list into song lyrics.

# 20-MINUTE PROMPT:

Cup your hands over your mouth and take a few breaths. Feel the moisture and warmth. Notice the sound made when you exhale. Drawing on this experience, write a movie scene with characters who wear surgical masks over their mouths. Keep dialogue to a minimum in this scene. Have breathing be the primary sound that is heard.

# Hello, Yellow

## 1-MINUTE PROMPT:

Sunshine, bananas, caution tape. They're all yellow, but they're not quite the same color, are they? Pick out something in your environment that's yellow. Pretend you've been given the job of naming this particular shade for a paint company. Create a list of possibilities, the more outrageous the better.

## 5-MINUTE PROMPT:

Is yellow the new black? Locate something yellow in your immediate surroundings. Imagine that an up-and-coming fashion designer is creating something for you in this very color. What does it look like? Write about what it's like to wear this during New York Fashion Week.

# 10-MINUTE PROMPT:

It turns out not everyone likes yellow. Your character has been asked to give a speech at the upcoming NOPWHY conference (National Organization of People Who Hate Yellow). After locating something yellow nearby, write down phrases and words to describe it. Use them in the opening lines of your character's speech.

# 20-MINUTE PROMPT:

What if you lived in a monochromatic world? Track down something yellow in your environment. Imagine that you wake up one morning to discover that the entire world has turned into that shade of yellow. Write a series of "Dear Diary" entries about what it's like trying to navigate this one-color world.

# Broken Places

## 1-MINUTE PROMPT:

Something in your environment has become damaged, be it a tangible object or an idea. Identify whatever it is then write a short obituary for That Which Is Broken.

## 5-MINUTE PROMPT:

There's a broken thing inside of you. Maybe it's something abstract like your heart. Maybe it's something concrete like your rib. Whatever it is, use it to create a character who is broken in the very same way. Discover how this broken thing changed the course of your character's life.

# 10-MINUTE PROMPT:

Something broken in your environment is suddenly the next DIY crafting craze. Figure out what it is then create a set of instructions for a crafting magazine detailing how to break this item in the oh-so-perfect way. Include suggestions on how to showcase this trendy item in one's home.

# 20-MINUTE PROMPT:

Cracks, tears, breaks, and rips. Brainstorm a list of all the broken things you see around you as well as those you find inside of yourself, be they physical, emotional, or otherwise. Write a short story that mentions each one of the items on your list.

# Can You Gimme a Hand with This?

## 1-MINUTE PROMPT:

Look at your hands. Notice the lines and wrinkles, the bony parts and the fleshy parts, perhaps even hardened calluses or missing fingers. Write a couple of detailed sentences that describe what you see.

## 5-MINUTE PROMPT:

Make a quick list of some of the ways you could use your hands right now. Then write about a romantic encounter between two characters that begins with one of them using their hands to do something mentioned on your list.

# 10-MINUTE PROMPT:

Love line or life line? Your character is a palm reader who's researching the history of palmistry. Using your own palms as reference, write about the meaning of these various lines on your hands.

# 20-MINUTE PROMPT:

A private investigator shows up at your door asking to see your hands. According to him your hands hold the key to solving a mystery. Look at your hands and find something—a tattoo, cracked nail polish, a birthmark, anything—and make that a clue. Write the dialogue between you and the investigator as you discuss the case and how your hands might fit into it.

# Look for the Signs

## 1-MINUTE PROMPT:

From product packaging to T-shirt slogans, words are all around you. Notice a word in your immediate environment. Write a complete three-sentence story—beginning, middle, and end—that includes that word.

## 5-MINUTE PROMPT:

You've got a bestseller in the works. *Hurrah!* Look around and find two words in your environment, be they in a magazine or on a billboard. Imagine a combination of those two words is the title of your new novel. Write a short summary about your upcoming release for the back of the book jacket.

# 10-MINUTE PROMPT:

Gather up all the words nearby. You know, the ones on the soup label, or discarded pamphlet, or billboard advertisement. Write them all down, then rearrange them to create a found poem.

# 20-MINUTE PROMPT:

In a dystopian future someone sends out an SOS message through a series of seemingly random words found in your environment. First, jot down words and phrases that you see around you. Next, write about what happens when your main character begins to piece these words together to uncover the distressed person's urgent message. What actions will your protagonist take next?

# Living Proof

## 1-MINUTE PROMPT:

*Ouch!* Once upon a time something unpleasant happened. It caused a physical scar on your body. Locate that scar and give it a good inspection. When you're finished, write about the scar's size, shape, texture, and quality.

## 5-MINUTE PROMPT:

Whether they've been accidentally pinched in a door or smashed with a hammer, your fingernails have been through some things. Take a gander at them right now, noticing the state they're in. Are they dirty? Are there any hangnails? Are your cuticles overgrown? Write a scene from a novel where a person contemplates his or her fingernails. Draw inspiration from the state of your own nails.

# 10-MINUTE PROMPT:

You're about to get some permanent ink to commemorate an important event. Take a good look at your skin. Where will the tattoo go and what will it be of? What event would you find meaningful enough that you'd be willing to get such a permanent reminder of it?

# 20-MINUTE PROMPT:

Wrinkles. They happen. We all get them. Open the camera app on your phone or find a mirror or reflective surface to look into. Inspect the wrinkles on your face and neck. Write a memoir excerpt connecting these wrinkles to various events in your life as though there was a cause-and-effect relationship between the two.

# The Sound and the Fury

## 1-MINUTE PROMPT:

*Shhh, listen!* There's an everyday noise you can hear right now that's part of a top-secret government experiment. What is the noise, and what experiment are they conducting?

## 5-MINUTE PROMPT:

"Can you repeat that?" Isolate two sounds happening in your environment. Write a scene where a couple tries to have a serious conversation, but the noises keep getting in the way.

# 10-MINUTE PROMPT:

A group of teenagers enter an abandoned house on a moonless night. They can't see much, but they can hear things. In fact, the sounds that you hear around you right now are the sounds they hear inside the dilapidated house. Describe the sounds and what happens when they walk through the house.

# 20-MINUTE PROMPT:

A man suffers from misophonia, a condition where hearing certain noises can trigger anger and other negative emotions. One of the noises you can hear right now is causing this man to become quite irritable. Write a stage play starring this feisty fellow. Include a monologue where he breaks the fourth wall and speaks directly to the audience about his ire.

# A Love Like No Other

## 1-MINUTE PROMPT:

The things around you are inanimate—or are they? Two objects in your environment are smitten with one another. One sends the other flowers. What does the message on the accompanying card read?

## 5-MINUTE PROMPT:

Pick two objects nearby. Imagine they experienced a spark of connection after briefly meeting in a shopping bag. Write a "missed connections" classified ad in the voice of one of these objects trying to find and woo the other.

# 10-MINUTE PROMPT:

Locate a visually pleasing thingamajig in your environment. What is it that makes it so attractive? Brainstorm a list of adjectives to describe this item, then use these words in a love poem written for someone who makes your heart beat a little faster.

# 20-MINUTE PROMPT:

Choose two everyday objects in your immediate environment. Imagine that two suitors attempt to win a princess's heart by bringing her these items as gifts. Write a scene from a fairy tale where the princess takes a good look at these gifts and decides whether to reject these suitors or not.

# You Wear It Well... Kinda

## 1-MINUTE PROMPT:

Whatever you've got on your feet—socks, shoes, slippers, and so on—has been taken away by the police as part of an ongoing investigation. What does the detective observe as she inspects these items and logs them into evidence?

## 5-MINUTE PROMPT:

After a short romance and subsequent Las Vegas wedding, a bride or groom meets their father-in-law for the first time while wearing the exact same shirt that you're now wearing. The new in-law is unhappy with the whirlwind wedding, but instead of addressing it head on, he's decided to pick on the shirt. Write the conversation between these two characters as they talk about this shirt. Use subtext to convey a deeper layer of meaning.

# 10-MINUTE PROMPT:

What are you wearing on your lower half? Whether it's pants, shorts, a skirt, or boxer briefs, write a colorful description of it for the Fashion History section of an online encyclopedia. Create some outlandish or fantastical details about things like the pattern designer, the thread used in the stitching, or the plants used to create the dye.

# 20-MINUTE PROMPT:

All the clothes you're wearing right now have been commandeered by the wardrobe supervisor of a high school drama department. The lead actor in tonight's production is wearing your outfit as his or her costume. What role is this actor playing? How are your clothes a perfect choice for that role?

# Survival Mode

## 1-MINUTE PROMPT:

Uh-oh. You're stranded in the wilderness without a phone, GPS device, or companion. Quickly choose an object in your environment that would be most useful to you in a survival situation. What is it about this object that makes it so important?

## 5-MINUTE PROMPT:

Your boat ran aground, and now you're marooned on an island. A tropical storm is about to pass over. You've got 20 minutes to build a shelter using only things you see in your environment. How durable and sturdy can you make it? Write about what it's like to be inside this makeshift shelter as the storm passes over.

# 10-MINUTE PROMPT:

A magazine has tapped you to write the true tale of a sailor who washed ashore after five years of being missing at sea. Choose a few items in your environment and imagine they were found in the sailor's boat. Write about how they contributed to the sailor's survival against all odds.

# 20-MINUTE PROMPT:

They thought it was only a snowstorm trapping them in the airport, but it's far worse than that. Now a family must use only the things found within an arm's length of where you're sitting or standing to fend off attackers until help arrives. Write about their struggle to stay alive during this travel nightmare.

# La La La La

## 1-MINUTE PROMPT:

How are you doing? Look within and make note of whether you're feeling content, bored, sad, elated, confused, irritable, or anything else. Write a couple lines of a blues song about your current emotional state.

## 5-MINUTE PROMPT:

A producer has asked you to compose a catchy chorus for a superstar's next hit song. Grab your phone or open your computer to find the last email or text message you sent. Use at least one of the words from your recent digital missive in the lyrics of this radio-friendly chorus.

# 10-MINUTE PROMPT:

Find a clothing label on something you're wearing. (You know, the one that says something like "See Reverse for Care.") Use the words on this label to write the lyrics to a simple country song. Consider the tone, whether it be sincere, darkly humorous, or sickly sweet.

# 20-MINUTE PROMPT:

What if your life was a theatrical production? Write a musical number about your day leading up to this very moment. Treat it, and what's happening around you, as if it were the pinnacle of an epic day, even—and especially—if everything's been relatively mundane so far.

# In My Not-So-Humble Opinion

## 1-MINUTE PROMPT:

Find something ho-hum that's happening in your environment right now, like a leaf blowing in the wind or a bus making a left-hand turn. You've been hired by a tabloid to write an outlandish tale about this typically minor event. Write down ideas for the sensational headline of this article.

## 5-MINUTE PROMPT:

We all know that Internet articles have dreadful characters in the comments section. Use your phone or computer to pull up an article about a current event. Perhaps it's a notable person's death, or a natural disaster, or an election scandal. Craft a pint-sized opinion piece in the style of an online comment about this event.

# 10-MINUTE PROMPT:

Locate a nearby newspaper or magazine and find an article or news item about a current event. If need be, pull up an article on your phone or computer. Re-envision this event as a modern-day fairy tale. Who are the villains? Who are the heroes? For fun, throw an accidental curse into your story.

# 20-MINUTE PROMPT:

The debate team is prepping for a regional event and you've got to argue one side of a divisive topic. Pick something in your environment that people could have a difference of opinion about, such as junk food or a skinny stretch of sidewalk. Next, write a debate speech defending your opinion on this potentially controversial subject.

# A Certain Kind of Atmosphere

## 1-MINUTE PROMPT:

Go to a window or step outside so you can look at the sky. What are the atmospheric conditions of temperature, wind, and cloud cover, if any? What is the quality of light? Write a haiku about the atmosphere.

## 5-MINUTE PROMPT:

There's the earth's physical atmosphere, and then there's a more abstract version of atmosphere that can best be described as *mood* or *vibe*. Taking both into consideration, write about the current atmosphere of your environment. What objects, colors, shapes, and spaces come together to create this atmosphere? How does the outside atmosphere affect your own mood and vibe?

# 10-MINUTE PROMPT:

You know air is all around you, despite the fact that you can't see it. But what if that changed? Imagine that, instead of being invisible, the air suddenly becomes dense and stringy. Visibility would be greatly reduced, and the atmosphere would surely shift. How would you navigate your way through the physical environment you're in right now? What would the air feel like on your skin now?

# 20-MINUTE PROMPT:

Take a peek outside. What are the current conditions? Consider air temperature, precipitation, and wind speed and direction. Write a scene from a thriller about a meteorologist who's murdered in the middle of writing a forecast. Include a reference to today's weather in your scene.

# Writing Sample

**1-MINUTE PROMPT:** Go to a window or step outside so you can look at the sky. What are the atmospheric conditions of temperature, wind, and cloud cover, if any? What is the quality of light? Write a haiku about the atmosphere.

**SAMPLE:**

Wide sky, blue expanse

Translucent clouds drift away

My skin, a cocoon

# Inner MacGyver

## 1-MINUTE PROMPT:

Chewing gum, paper clips, and shoelaces are all potential DIY tools that a crafty person could use in a pinch. Find an item on your person or nearby that, with a little rejiggering, could be fashioned into a makeshift tool. What is it, and how would you use it?

## 5-MINUTE PROMPT:

An off-duty firefighter happens upon a burning house and hears screams coming from within. Look around your environment. What can the firefighter use to smash a window or break down a door in order to get inside? How does it help or hinder his rescue effort?

# 10-MINUTE PROMPT:

A thief is looking for something to break into a stolen, padlocked box. Write a short story from the point of view of this criminal who's using an object that's near you right now to try and smash the lock. Is the thief successful? If so, what's inside the box?

# 20-MINUTE PROMPT:

Everything has its own purpose and intended use, but what about unintended uses? Choose a variety of things in your environment and come up with alternative uses for them, such as turning a pencil into a cocktail stirrer. Create a *Journal of Alternate Uses* that names the objects and lists various ways they can be used.

# I'm No Slouch

## 1-MINUTE PROMPT:

Whether you're sitting, standing, or lying down, take stock of your posture at the moment. How is your spine curved, compressed, stretched? Are your shoulders hunched or pulled back? Write the opening lines of a novel introducing your main character in the same pose you're currently in.

## 5-MINUTE PROMPT:

Wherever you have mobility, move your body a little bit. You might shift your weight from side to side, tilt your neck, stretch your back and arms, or rock side to side. Remember the order of these movements, then imagine that they're actually part of a choreographed dance. Write notes on the dance from the point of view of the choreographer.

# 10-MINUTE PROMPT:

Feel your spine from the base of your neck to the bottom of your tailbone. Make note of any sensations, areas of tension, and places where you're flexible or inflexible. As though your spine has its own voice, write an inner monologue where it talks about supporting your body.

# 20-MINUTE PROMPT:

A burnt-out copywriter has an assignment to produce the ad copy for a chiropractor's marketing materials. Instead of doing the appropriate research, the copywriter decides to make it all up, including fake quotes by doctors and patients. Use your own posture as reference point to write this bogus text about spines and back health.

# All the News That's Unfit to Print

## 1-MINUTE PROMPT:

You're a freelance journalist and you need ideas for stories. Look at what's around you and use what you find as inspiration for a story idea that you can pitch to a media outlet.

## 5-MINUTE PROMPT:

Find a person in your environment. If there's not an actual person nearby find one on TV, in a magazine, or on a billboard. Create a news story about that person for tonight's evening news.

# 10-MINUTE PROMPT:

All kinds of things are happening around you. They might be as compelling as an ambulance racing by or as uneventful as a dog taking a nap. Create a series of *Twitter* updates giving the blow-by-blow account of everything that occurs in the next 10 minutes.

# 20-MINUTE PROMPT:

A news reporter sticks a microphone in your face. Write a scene where you're being interviewed about what you're doing right now. Then grab the mic and interview her. What do you ask that gets her to reveal a secret about herself live on the air?

# As Above, So Below

## 1-MINUTE PROMPT:

Imagine that what's above you—whether it's the ceiling or the sky—is now below you. What would it be like to walk across this terrain? Are there light fixtures or skylights to avoid? Are there telephone wires you might get tangled in? Describe the dreamlike and surreal experience.

## 5-MINUTE PROMPT:

A tornado touches down in the location you're in right now. It turns everything upside down. After it passes through what's the first thing you see? What objects, people, or animals have been affected by this disaster?

# 10-MINUTE PROMPT:

Alarms sound. Police officers yell instructions through megaphones. Phones ring incessantly. It turns out that scientists have discovered an imminent shift in gravity. Within the next 20 minutes the world might, quite literally, turn upside down. Your main character needs to make some quick decisions. Open the scene with your protagonist standing wherever you are, then figure out what happens next. Will this person run for shelter? Try to meet up with loved ones? Frantically look for a way to stop this?

# 20-MINUTE PROMPT:

A teenager's world has been flipped upside down—literally. Examine the sky or ceiling above you and look at the ground or floor below you. Using your environment as a reference point, write about this teenager's experience in this new upside-down reality. Consider that this literal flip is related to a more abstract emotional "flip" she's recently experienced. See if you can connect the dots between these two flips in an interesting and clever way.

# Alphabetically Speaking

## 1-MINUTE PROMPT:

Something nearby begins with the letter *D*. Write the name of it vertically, so that each letter starts off a new sentence. For example, if the word is *dish* the first sentence begins with a *D* word, and the second sentence begins with an *I* word, and so on.

## 5-MINUTE PROMPT:

Look around for an object that begins with the letter *C* or the letter *E*. That word is now the title of your new movie script. First determine the genre, then write a plot summary about it for an industry magazine.

# 10-MINUTE PROMPT:

Name all the things nearby that begin with the letter *T* or *S*. These are the items on someone's shopping list. Write a scene where this character tries to track down and purchase these things, but various obstacles get in the way.

# 20-MINUTE PROMPT:

Make a list of everything in your environment that begins with the letter *R*, *U*, or *N*. Use those words in a scene from a zombie story where the protagonist has a broken leg and is forced to run through the pain in order to escape.

# 1-MINUTE PROMPT:

Find something that you can count only one of in your immediate surroundings. Write the first page of a children's picture book that uses this singular thing to teach kids about the number one.

# 5-MINUTE PROMPT:

Find a pair of identical things in your surroundings. Compose a classified "For Sale" ad trying to sell this pair. Try to pinpoint their best qualities to entice a buyer.

# 10-MINUTE PROMPT:

Find three things in your environment that look alike. Mention them in a short essay you write about the significance of the number three. Whether you approach this from a mathematical, mystical, visual, or other point of view, see if you can include other well-known trios in this essay.

# 20-MINUTE PROMPT:

Find four things nearby that appear to be identical to one another on first glance but are actually quite unique in their own ways (such as four petals on a flower, or four hairs on a cat). Do some freestyle writing about these things starting with the subtle differences between each one. Then take that writing and create a work that contains four parts or paragraphs of prose.

# The Skin I'm In

## 1-MINUTE PROMPT:

Can you appreciate what you've got? Look into a mirror (or reflective surface) or use your phone's camera app to check yourself out. Write about something you see that evokes a feeling of gratitude, however subtle.

## 5-MINUTE PROMPT:

Make a list of words related to the physical quality of your skin (e.g., smooth, wrinkled, freckled), then create a rhyming poem using words on your list.

# 10-MINUTE PROMPT:

The pigmentation of one's skin is an incredibly complex topic. Imagine you've been asked to write an essay for a high-profile magazine about the relationship you have to the color of your skin and the relationship that society has with it. Look at your skin as you write this piece. See if anything about its physical aspects may be included in the essay.

# 20-MINUTE PROMPT:

Skin is biology. There's the epidermis and dermis, blood vessels, hair follicles, and fatty tissue too. Take a moment to feel the skin on your legs. Poke at it. Scratch it lightly. Imagine there's a scraping of your skin on a glass slide in a dermatologist's research lab. Include a brief description of it in a series of research reports written by this dermatologist. When read consecutively, these reports tell the story of a peculiar discovery the dermatologist has made about your skin.

# Spellbound

## 1-MINUTE PROMPT:

The power is within you. But it's also outside of you, because something in your environment is a talisman with ancient magical powers. What is it and what kind of magic does it help to create?

## 5-MINUTE PROMPT:

Think carefully. You can cast one magic spell to permanently alter something in your environment. What would it be, and why?

# 10-MINUTE PROMPT:

Boom! You've been turned into a powerful wizard and everything you see around you is part of your enchanted lair. Create a recipe for a spell that utilizes things you can see around you. What will your spell work on? What's the incantation you must chant when using this spell?

# 20-MINUTE PROMPT:

Your character comes from a long line of healers known for their potent elixirs and healing spells. One of the objects in your environment is the most powerful tool in the healer's arsenal, and it needs protection from thieves who wish to sell it on the black market. How does your character evade these thieves and smuggle this object to safety?

# Soundscape

## 1-MINUTE PROMPT:

Pause. Listen to your surroundings. Hone in on one sound. Try to capture its quality and rhythm using phonetic spelling and descriptive language.

## 5-MINUTE PROMPT:

Listen. What do you hear? Pick one sound and imagine it's the very last time that sound will be heard on planet Earth. Write a goodbye to this sound in the form of an obituary.

# 10-MINUTE PROMPT:

Make noises. With a pen. With your phone. With your hands. Scratch, bonk, tap, clap. Create a dictionary of sounds you can manufacture right now. Do your best to describe them phonetically. Feel free to make up words.

# 20-MINUTE PROMPT:

Quickly jot down a list of sounds you can hear in your environment. Then write a short movie script about two characters who fall in love, even though they can only speak to each other with these sounds. Does this romance end tragically or can it endure?

# Writing Sample

**10-MINUTE PROMPT:** Make noises. With a pen. With your phone. With your hands. Scratch, bonk, tap, clap. Create a dictionary of sounds you can manufacture right now. Do your best to describe them phonetically. Feel free to make up words.

**SAMPLE:**

Tink Tink: The sound of a plastic pen tapping against a glass table.

Crrr-Crrr-Chhh: The noise made when caressing the dried leaves of a fern plant.

Tadatadatadatada: The sound of fingernails rapidly drumming on the tabletop.

Tok-Tok: The rhythmic tapping together of two seashells, one a scallop shell and the other a moon snail shell.

Ttttttttt: The subtle yet annoying sound of the ceramic bowl as it rattles against the table every time you start typing, but you're too lazy to move it.

Schika Schika Schika: The noise made when you rub your flattened palms together in a back-and-forth manner like a villain.

Wheesho Wheesho Wheesho: The noise made when you rub your flattened palms together in a circular manner like a person who's really cold.

Tang-Tong: The hollow metallic sounds produced by two alternating feet tapping on the steel base of a table, which is kind of rusty and you really should try to fix that up.

O-o-o-p-p-p-t-t-h-h-h-h: The noise you hear inside your head when slowly slurping coffee from a paper cup through a partially closed mouth. (Not to be confused with AAGGGHHH, a noise you make when forced to listen to someone else slurping coffee.)

# Personal Effects

## 1-MINUTE PROMPT:

Pull out your pocketbook, wallet, briefcase, or book bag. Without looking, reach in and take one item from it. Imagine this item was left behind at the place where a missing person was last seen. Compose the inner monologue of someone who finds this item at the scene of the disappearance.

## 5-MINUTE PROMPT:

Choose three random items from inside your pocketbook, wallet, briefcase, or book bag. These three items have been unearthed in a time capsule. Who buried this capsule and what were they trying to tell the world about themselves?

# 10-MINUTE PROMPT:

Your character has been summoned to a lawyer's office to be told he's the sole inheritor of an unknown relative's estate. His inheritance consists entirely of the contents of your briefcase, pocketbook, wallet, or book bag. Write the dialogue between your character and the probate lawyer as they look through this random assortment of items.

# 20-MINUTE PROMPT:

You're on a camping trip with a group of scouts. As scout leader it's practically mandatory for you to tell a spooky story to the kids gathered around the campfire. Create a suspense-filled tall tale about something unusual that lives in the woods. Be sure to feature items found in your pocketbook, wallet, briefcase, or book bag in the story.

# Choose Wisely

## 1-MINUTE PROMPT:

You're a CIA operative who has to plant a listening device nearby. You must choose someplace inconspicuous or your cover will be blown. Write about where you discreetly hide the device.

## 5-MINUTE PROMPT:

The folks from the TV show *Antiques Roadshow* are in town. There's one item in your environment that can fetch a pretty penny at auction. What item could it be? What do the appraisers say about it when you show them? Write the scene where they help you uncover the true history of this unlikely valuable item.

# 10-MINUTE PROMPT:

A genie has granted you the opportunity to keep one thing in your environment without any consequence, even if it's something that currently belongs to someone else. Write about your decision-making process. Consider, if what you choose belongs to someone else now, whether you'll have any feelings of guilt or remorse later.

# 20-MINUTE PROMPT:

A doctor holds an x-ray up to the light. It seems to indicate that the patient has swallowed a foreign object. Pick an item in your environment and make it the object seen on the scan. Do you choose something that's, um, easy to pass, or something that requires emergency surgery? Write a scene between the ER doctor and patient as they discuss the next steps. Include the patient's explanation as to why he or she swallowed the object in the first place.

# Touchy-Feely

## 1-MINUTE PROMPT:

Locate something nearby that's too large to hold, like a tree or an apartment building. Imagine you could actually pick it up and run your hand along its surfaces. What would it feel like?

## 5-MINUTE PROMPT:

Locate something nearby that has a soft texture. Then locate something soft within you. Write about these two kinds of softness, one physical and one more abstract.

# 10-MINUTE PROMPT:

Find something with a physically bumpy texture in your environment. Think of a memory or experience you once had that could be described as emotionally bumpy. Write a free verse poem about these two kinds of bumpiness.

# 20-MINUTE PROMPT:

There are smooth things in your environment and jagged things. Make note of them. Consider that there are smooth or jagged things inside of you, be they memories, emotions, or physical attributes. Make note of those too. Use your observations on these tangible and intangible smooth and jagged things to create the backstory of a complex character. How did this character become so complicated? What motivates this character? What makes this character angry? What is this character's mission in life?

# A Better Place

## 1-MINUTE PROMPT:

Suppose you can make the world a better place in one itty-bitty way—by taking something ugly in your environment and making it attractive. What is it and how could you beautify it?

## 5-MINUTE PROMPT:

Sometimes a small repair is all that's needed on something broken. Other times, the job is a beast of a project. Find something in disrepair nearby, no matter how big or small, and envision the process of fixing it up. Would it make any real difference to the world? Would repairing it bring you satisfaction or might you actually prefer it in its worn-out state? Write a diary entry about the implications of fixing this thing.

# 10-MINUTE PROMPT:

Things get dirty. That's just a fact of life. But what if they didn't have to? Imagine a superhero whose mission it is to keep the world clean and their nemesis who delights in making things dirty. Look around and make note of what's clean and what's dirty nearby. Write the text from a comic book scene where these two characters struggle to gain a foothold in your environment.

# 20-MINUTE PROMPT:

Philosophically speaking, how would you make the location you're in a better place? It could be as simple as installing more water bowls for thirsty dogs or as complicated as installing more UN peacekeepers to stabilize the region. Contemplate your surroundings and write about the ways you'd make this little corner of the world a better place.

# Can I Get a Witness?

## 1-MINUTE PROMPT:

Let's test your powers of observation. Find an object nearby and study it for 10 seconds. Without looking at it again, write about it with as much detail as possible.

## 5-MINUTE PROMPT:

How well can you remember what's around you? Take a quick scan of your environment then answer these questions as accurately as possible: What is to your left? What is to your right? What's in front of you? What's behind you? If you're in a location that you're very familiar with, such as your home, try to include extra details in your descriptions.

# 10-MINUTE PROMPT:

Find something nearby that's moving, whether it's a truck that's backing up or a bird flitting through the trees. Study the movement for a minute. When finished, imagine you've been asked to write a detailed witness statement about what you saw. Consider color, size, shape, distance, and any other relevant information as you write your recollections.

# 20-MINUTE PROMPT:

Answer the following questions as best you can without looking up or around. Ready? What in your environment is the color gray? What is round or circular in shape? What area is most brightly lit? What area has the darkest shadow? Use these answers to craft a courtroom scene where a lawyer is cross-examining an eyewitness to a crime.

# Building Blocks

## 1-MINUTE PROMPT:

Locate a building in your line of sight. It may be out the window or in the pages of a nearby magazine. Write about the style and look of the building.

## 5-MINUTE PROMPT:

Realtors are always talking about "good bones." What if the building you're inside of (or one you can see nearby) had an actual skeletal structure to it? Write about the building from an anatomical perspective.

# 10-MINUTE PROMPT:

Brick, wood, cement, metal, and stone are just some of the materials that might be used in the construction of a building. Whether it's the building you're inside of right now or a building nearby, write a scene from a musical with two workers singing about the material they're using to construct the building.

# 20-MINUTE PROMPT:

You're a famous architect in town for a conference. Write a speech to present to the other architects about your latest project. Be sure to slip in the words *façade* and *motif*. Use the building you're in now or a building you can see nearby as a model for the architect's new venture.

# Worrier Mode

## 1-MINUTE PROMPT:

Pause and reflect on a worry you currently have, even if it's as minor as wondering whether your parking meter has run out. When you think about this worry what sensations happen in your body? Write about them.

## 5-MINUTE PROMPT:

Officials from the Department of Concerns and Worries are here for their annual audit. Make a complete inventory list of your current worries and concerns. If the list seems flimsy, feel free to add the worries of your friends and family. Give each worry on the list a title and a one-sentence summary.

# 10-MINUTE PROMPT:

Look around. Find something in your environment that could cause you, or someone else, to worry. Make this worry the primary concern of your main character. Write about this character's session with a therapist as they discuss this worry.

# 20-MINUTE PROMPT:

Right now, think of a teeny, tiny concern you currently have. Something like chipped nail polish or a pen that doesn't work anymore. Imagine now that this barely there concern is actually a huge problem for someone else. In fact, this tiny concern of yours is a life-or-death situation for your character. Write about this person's tenuous struggle.

# Zoom Out

## 1-MINUTE PROMPT:

What do you look like from above? Imagine that you are a character in a novel and the narrator is seeing you from the vantage point of hovering ten feet above. What does the narrator observe about you and your immediate surroundings?

## 5-MINUTE PROMPT:

Imagine a drone with a video camera is flying forty feet above you. (If you're indoors imagine the roof has been removed from the building or that it's, perhaps, invisible.) Write about the space around you and how you would appear from a wider vantage point. Perhaps the drone sees things you're not able to see, such as a car pulling onto the street or a hawk perched on a branch nearby.

# 10-MINUTE PROMPT:

A pilot is flying over you a mile high in the sky. What would this person see when they peered down on you? Imagine how your town or city would look from above right now, what parts of the neighborhood would be bustling with activity and what parts would be quiet. Write about this aerial perspective and your place within it.

# 20-MINUTE PROMPT:

Unbeknownst to you, the International Space Station is passing over your part of the world right now. Think of everything around you—the land, the sky, the environment—and what it might look like from far above. Write a story about an astronaut looking down on you, even if neither one of you is aware of it. Highlight the dynamic push and pull between the perspectives of someone who is earthbound and someone who is floating through space looking down on the earth's landscape.

# (2)

# IMAGINATION PROMPTS

Your ripe and willing creative mind is all that you need to work with the Imagination Prompts. That means the possibilities of what may arise as a result are boundless. Whether it's dreaming up a fantastical scenario or making fresh connections between seemingly unrelated things, your mind is like an oversized treasure chest just waiting to be opened, unpacked, and marveled over. While many of the Imagination Prompts are suited to fiction writers, there are also plenty of prompts for writers with nonfiction interests. Both playfulness *and* critical thinking are possible when using these prompts—and (as a reminder) these two things are not necessarily exclusive to one another. As you delve into the Imagination Prompts you'll notice the elasticity of your creative mind. That stretchy, rubberlike quality will surely help you envision new worlds, unique characters, and original ideas. If you complete all of the prompts in this section and find yourself wanting to use them over again, simply mix and match some of the parameters, such as swapping up genres or writing styles or tweaking some of the details or concepts. Anything goes!

# Over the River and to the Gas Station

## 1-MINUTE PROMPT:

Little Red Riding Hood hides out in the bathroom stall of a gas station. The Big Bad Wolf pounds on the door. How does she escape?

## 5-MINUTE PROMPT:

On the way to Granny's house Little Red Riding Hood stops at the local gas station to grab snacks for her basket. As she contemplates her choices a mysterious man with a wolf tattoo engages her in conversation. Write the tense dialogue between them.

# 10-MINUTE PROMPT:

Local celebrity Little Red Riding Hood is spotted pumping gas without her signature cape. Unnamed sources say she's vowed never to wear the color red again. Write a breaking news report for tonight's TV broadcast about this developing situation.

# 20-MINUTE PROMPT:

While working as a gas station attendant Little Red Riding Hood hears that the Wolf is getting paroled twenty years after trying to murder her and Granny. Create a three-act play about Little Red Riding Hood receiving this news and the struggle to come to terms with what the Wolf's release might mean for her life.

# Hear Ye, Hear Ye

## 1-MINUTE PROMPT:

*Aisle, isle,* and *I'll* are three words that sound alike but have very different meanings. Use all three of them in a micropoem meant to be read aloud at an open mic poetry slam.

## 5-MINUTE PROMPT:

The word *right* has several different meanings and sounds exactly like the words *rite* and *write*. Craft a robust paragraph that uses all three of these same-sounding words, along with two different meanings for the word *right*.

# 10-MINUTE PROMPT:

Your main character is a wordsmith who's often misunderstood by others. Write the conversation between your protagonist and another person who's confused by the wordsmith's use of the same-sounding words *rays, raise,* and *raze.*

# 20-MINUTE PROMPT:

*Prays, praise,* and *preys* couldn't have more dissimilar meanings from one another, despite the fact that they sound exactly alike. Use all three words in a short horror story that takes place in a sleepy town more than a hundred years ago. Who is praying, and who is preying? Who or what is being praised?

# Tick Tock, Tick Tock

## 1-MINUTE PROMPT:

From the eighth-story window of a high-rise building you can see that a child meanders along the train tracks as a fast-moving bullet train approaches. Fortunately, you have a secret power that will save the child's life. Write about it.

## 5-MINUTE PROMPT:

In the middle of a remote country field, a barely conscious person is stuck at the bottom of a well. Then the heavy rain begins, and the well water rises. What happens next? Will the person save themselves or will they perish?

# 10-MINUTE PROMPT:

You're on a film set watching your screenplay come to life as a thriller. The producer asks you to pen an additional scene where a new SWAT team member must unarm a ticking bomb while navigating her own nerves. Get that scene nailed down before the director yells "Action!" again.

# 20-MINUTE PROMPT:

Your character has been told by doctors that his condition is untreatable, and he only has hours left to live. Through a twist of fate, he learns there's actually a cure—now all he needs to do is get to it before time runs out. Where is this cure? How can your character get to it in time?

# Fight or Flight

## 1-MINUTE PROMPT:

What is a bird without its ability to fly? Your character is a birder who has spied an avian friend with a broken wing. In the style of a birding journal entry write down the birder's observations about the bird's predicament.

## 5-MINUTE PROMPT:

A bird with social anxiety receives an invite to a party thrown by a neighborhood flock and doesn't feel comfortable declining it. The bird must navigate small talk and conversation at the shindig while trying to keep anxiety in check. It's all going pretty well, until the bird's fight-or-flight response kicks in.

# 10-MINUTE PROMPT:

Imagine a time in your life when you felt like a bird with no wings. With rich detail, describe your experience as a bird in the state of being wingless. Write it as an excerpt from a novel that has fantasy elements.

# 20-MINUTE PROMPT:

Think of two birds of differing species with opposite attributes. Create short character studies for each that include physical descriptions and real or imagined behaviors and personality traits. Then, using those studies for reference, write a fight scene between these two birds that doesn't rely on dialogue or inner monologue. Consider how the birds' differences may have caused the conflict.

# No Place Like Home

## 1-MINUTE PROMPT:

Home is more than a geographical or physical location. It's also a feeling. Write about the primary emotion that surfaces when you think about home.

## 5-MINUTE PROMPT:

Think of a place where you once lived. Ideally, it's a home you haven't seen in a while, a place that isn't a part of your day-to-day reality, a place that no longer houses your belongings or hosts your beloved visitors. Write this former home a funeral song to honor its place in your life.

# 10-MINUTE PROMPT:

Spend a few minutes brainstorming a list of words that describe home. Consider the architectural structure of your dwelling as well as the feelings and energy of the space. Use all of these words in a poem. When finished find a phrase within the poem to be used as the title for the piece.

# 20-MINUTE PROMPT:

On moving day, a couple of senior citizens take one last walk through the home they shared together for decades. Write about the memories that arise as they meander through. Consider whether they feel melancholy, hopeful, angry, confused, relieved, or, perhaps, some combination of those emotions. What are some of the experiences they had when living in this home?

# Oh Thread Count, My Thread Count

## 1-MINUTE PROMPT:

An insomniac who hasn't slept in weeks climbs into bed at the end of the day. Pen some lyrics to a lullaby that this person sings to themselves.

## 5-MINUTE PROMPT:

A man who's been hospitalized after an accident is hallucinating terrible things, things that want him dead. Write a short horror tale based on the wild visions of this bed-ridden man who's fighting for his life.

# 10-MINUTE PROMPT:

Sleep. We all do it, and yet the experience of it varies from person to person. Write a short essay about sleep for an online news site. Choose the angle you want to approach the article from, be it clinical, metaphoric, poetic, physiological, personal, or some combo of those.

# 20-MINUTE PROMPT:

Little-known fact: the Guardian of the Night Realm watches over you in your sleep. Choose a main character and write about this person's fantastical experience meeting the Guardian. Is the Guardian benevolent or malevolent? What is the Guardian's purpose in this character's dream state?

# Stirring the Pot

## 1-MINUTE PROMPT:

What if there were an actual Recipe for Love? Choose a particular kind of love (unconditional, unrequited, maternal, or puppy, for example) and create a list of ingredients for this recipe.

## 5-MINUTE PROMPT:

What does success mean to you? Create an actual Recipe for Success for a conceptual cookbook that's going to be marketed to creative types. What ingredients would work in combination to equal artistic success? How much of each ingredient is needed?

# 10-MINUTE PROMPT:

During the creation of the universe a Supreme Being tasks you with making an actual Recipe for Disaster. Include a list of ingredients and the amounts used of each, as well as step-by-step instructions for combining ingredients—whether they be baked, fried, or flambéed. Be sure to mention any variations on the recipe.

# 20-MINUTE PROMPT:

Since you're a big-city food writer in high demand, all the celebrity chefs want you to write the introduction to their new cookbooks. Pick one that highlights the latest trendy ingredient on the foodie scene, then write an introduction that wows everyone with your (potentially fictionalized) knowledge of this ingredient and its uses. Make mention of one of the chef's recipes in the intro.

# L.E.T.T.E.R.S.

## 1-MINUTE PROMPT:

Who needs all twenty-six letters when three will do you just fine? Take a stab at writing a few sentences using only words that begin with the letters *N, U,* and *I.*

## 5-MINUTE PROMPT:

*T Is for Tabloid* is the title of your new satirical kids' book for adults based on the letters of the alphabet. What irreverent, scandalous, or sensational things do the other letters stand for?

# 10-MINUTE PROMPT:

What does unity mean to you? Write a five-line poem with the letters *U*, *N*, *I*, *T*, and *Y* within each line so that the word *UNITY* can be read on the vertical axis of the piece. Don't feel that this poem has to be flush left. Instead, play around with its shape on the page.

# 20-MINUTE PROMPT:

Spend 2 minutes freewriting about anything that comes into your mind. Don't worry if it's interesting or even makes a lot of sense. When finished, go back through the writing and edit it to remove all the *R*s, *N*s, *I*s, *S*s, and *Y*s. Write a scene where a character walks past a cordoned-off crime scene and finds a note with this strange altered text. What does this person do next?

# Writing Sample

**1-MINUTE PROMPT:** Who needs all twenty-six letters when three will do you just fine? Take a stab at writing a few sentences using only words that begin with the letters *N*, *U*, and *I*.

## SAMPLE:

Ugh, undulating undead never not napping. Unreal nervousness under nimble umbrellas! Irksome unrest, irritable upset. No, not normal, is it?

# Clanging and Banging

## 1-MINUTE PROMPT:

Imagine the noise generated the moment a tornado rips through a salvage yard. Describe the symphonic cacophony.

## 5-MINUTE PROMPT:

A person sees his ex for the first time since breaking up. It seems his heart might bang right out of his chest. The noise grows so loud that others start to notice. Will his ex hear it too?

# 10-MINUTE PROMPT:

In medieval times two knights wearing armor have lost their swords in battle and now they've taken to wrestling. Write a sonically rich piece focusing on the clash of metal on metal as these two grapple for victory.

# 20-MINUTE PROMPT:

A person's organs have been replaced by gears and machine parts. Suddenly, one of the parts grinds to a halt. Describe the sound of the working part as it peters out, then write about this person's visit to the mechanic. Include mention of a stethoscope and other tools that the mechanic uses for diagnosis and treatment.

# Well, That Escalated Quickly

## 1-MINUTE PROMPT:

Splash! Gasp! Using short, efficient sentences, write a tiny theatrical play that ends with one character suddenly throwing a drink in another character's face.

## 5-MINUTE PROMPT:

Everything seemed to be going so well at the big family reunion. Next thing you know, someone trips someone else by accident and—Bam!—a brawl ensues. Who are the two characters fighting? How does it get broken up?

# 10-MINUTE PROMPT:

A pair of horses is tied up outside a saloon. Two pistols are drawn. A clock strikes high noon. These images have all the makings of a classic Western showdown. But this isn't the American Southwest. It's not even planet Earth. Write about this duel that takes place elsewhere in the cosmos.

# 20-MINUTE PROMPT:

Two skydivers jump out of a plane. One of them quickly discovers that her backpack doesn't contain a parachute, but something else entirely. Write a screenplay scene describing the clash between the skydiver and her antagonist as they tumble toward Earth.

# Gone Missing

## 1-MINUTE PROMPT:

A random acquaintance from an online social network has gone missing. For some reason this person has chosen to send a cryptic three-line email to you. What does it say?

## 5-MINUTE PROMPT:

After receiving a cryptic three-line message from a missing acquaintance you must place an ad in the local paper for a detective. What does the ad say?

# 10-MINUTE PROMPT:

You're interviewing detectives-for-hire so they can help you track down a person you haven't seen in years. Write a movie montage scene showcasing the motley cast of characters who want the job.

# 20-MINUTE PROMPT:

Police bring you to a location that's very familiar to you where they've uncovered a huge clue in the mystery of a missing acquaintance—your own house. Write the scene and include reference to a dark secret from your past.

# Takeout Tales

## 1-MINUTE PROMPT:

Your stomach rumbles. You're eager to dive into your takeout dinner. You open one of the containers and find something quite unexpected inside. What is it and how do you react?

## 5-MINUTE PROMPT:

"Oh Lo Mein, Lo Mein! Wherefore art thou Lo Mein?" Who among us hasn't fallen head over heels for the sweet convenience of takeout food? Imagine Shakespeare has received his first ever delivery of takeout food. Write a sketch comedy skit of the banter between the famous writer and the delivery person.

# 10-MINUTE PROMPT:

After a long night of work, a pizza delivery person orders takeout food and discovers that the person delivering his food is...himself. How is that possible? What happens next?

# 20-MINUTE PROMPT:

A notable magazine has hired you to pen an article about the changing culture of takeout food. Choose an angle for the piece, such as the quality or type of food, the way restaurants are gaining or losing new customers, or, perhaps, the use of technology in delivery methods. Include some made-up statistics, quotes, and factoids (or, if you have time, bolster your article with factual research).

# Oh So High in the Sky

## 1-MINUTE PROMPT:

What does it mean to soar through the sky or flap your wings through an intense gust of wind? Write a page for a children's book about the imagined experience of flying.

## 5-MINUTE PROMPT:

Folklore is a tradition that uses fictional stories to explain something about the world. Write a short folk tale that explains how birds got their wings. Include a detailed description of bird feathers somewhere in your tale.

# 10-MINUTE PROMPT:

Only those with wings can exist in the Air Realm. Dragons, witches, angels, and fairies all consort in this fantastical place. For the most part, everyone gets along fine here, but occasionally there's a kerfuffle—and, unfortunately, kerfuffles can lead to war. Write about the rising tension between inhabitants of the Air Realm as war approaches.

# 20-MINUTE PROMPT:

*Hey, you can fly! Pretty cool, man.* A magazine has asked you to write a "How To" about your aerial ability. Write a short introduction to the instructional, then the steps that describe how a person can achieve liftoff.

# Dust Bunnies and Cobwebs

## 1-MINUTE PROMPT:

A single woman enters her home and notices right away that her housekeeper never cleaned as promised. What did the woman see that tipped her off to this?

## 5-MINUTE PROMPT:

You're a housekeeper for a busy exec. An odd noise interrupts your usual cleaning routine. You put down your vacuum to go investigate. What you find shocks you. Write a "Dear Diary" entry about your discovery.

# 10-MINUTE PROMPT:

A tired restaurant manager arrives home after work and is surprised to see his housekeeper's car in the driveway. Inside, he finds the house only partially cleaned and discovers a series of clues that lead him to believe that the housekeeper has succumbed to foul play. Write about these clues as he pieces them together.

# 20-MINUTE PROMPT:

On the day she's laid off from her job, a professor arrives home to find a ransom note left by kidnappers who claim to have taken her beloved housekeeper. The ransom note reads like a long, strange poem. It's written in rhyme and contains a riddle. What does it say?

# Story of My Life

## 1-MINUTE PROMPT:

Imagine your life is an actual, hold-it-in-your-hands book. Give the story of your existence thus far a rating of between one and five stars and add a review that explains why. (Reminder: be gentle with yourself—it's just a prompt!)

## 5-MINUTE PROMPT:

One player or two? Imagine your life is a video game that someone could pick up and play. What are the challenges that players would have to overcome as they navigate the terrain of your life? Where can they earn extra points along the way?

# 10-MINUTE PROMPT:

*Roll credits!* Imagine your life is a movie. What genre would it be? What's the big plot twist? Who would you want to direct it and why? What would it be rated?

# 20-MINUTE PROMPT:

What if your life was a concept album? Create a list of the songs featured on it and give each a brief description. Write down ideas you have for the album cover and think of who you want to thank in the liner notes.

# Amen and Hallelujah

## 1-MINUTE PROMPT:

Someone receives good news that brings them to their knees. Write a line or two of dialogue as this person expresses joy, shock, or disbelief at what they've just heard.

## 5-MINUTE PROMPT:

Some people go to church and some go to the woods. Think of a place where you feel connected to something bigger or something deeper and use that location as a backdrop for a scene that has only one character in it. (One human character, that is.)

# 10-MINUTE PROMPT:

In a post-apocalyptic world, prayer is commodified and dispensed in capsule form. Salvation is readily available to those with the most wealth. For all the rest, there's the black market. Write a scene that takes place during a stealthy black market transaction. Who's trying to cultivate more faith, and who's got some to sell?

# 20-MINUTE PROMPT:

Let's say you're given the opportunity to start your own church—any kind of church. Maybe the worship revolves around a known deity, or maybe it revolves around a less common form of spiritual upliftment, such as the annual arrival of a migrating bird. First, decide who or what this church will be dedicated to, then give it a good name. Once that's done, compose the sermon that you'll give to your congregation on opening day.

# Fake News

## 1-MINUTE PROMPT:

Do you often tell the whole truth and nothing but the truth, or not? Imagine you're an expert on something that you actually know nothing about. Create a fictitious factoid about the topic.

## 5-MINUTE PROMPT:

*Well, la dee da!* A magazine that profiles highly influential people wants to do a cover story on you. Create an outlandish synopsis of your life so you can send it along to the journalist assigned to the story.

# 10-MINUTE PROMPT:

Zzzzz. What are some ho-hum personality traits you consider to be serious snoozefest material? Imagine a satire website has hired you to write a piece poking fun at a famous person who exhibits these yawn-inducing traits.

# 20-MINUTE PROMPT:

Write down the first three animals that pop into your head. Pretend you're a paleontologist who's just discovered the bones of a new species of dinosaur resembling some combination of these three animals. Write about your career-changing discovery—without forgetting to give it an official-sounding name—and include mention of where the skeleton was found and how you and your team knew to look there.

# Building Blocks

**NOTE:** *each of these prompts builds on the previous one, so start with the 1-minute prompt and go from there.*

# 1-MINUTE PROMPT:

Quick! Set the timer and go! Don't think too much; just let the words tumble out. If the writing seems disjointed or even nonsensical, you're on the right track. Save what you wrote to do the next prompt when ready.

# 5-MINUTE PROMPT:

Grab the writing you did from the previous prompt. Extract any interesting two- and three-word pairings. Keeping them in their original order, add text between and around these snippets to create a narrative. Save this for the next prompt.

# 10-MINUTE PROMPT:

Imagine that a character is sneaking a look at the diary of a loved one. The page that this person is reading contains your writing from the 5-minute prompt. Take an excerpt from that writing and use it as a starting point to this scene that explores the character's reaction to what's on the page. Consider how this information may affect this character's relationship with the person who wrote it.

# 20-MINUTE PROMPT:

Take your writing from the 10-minute prompt and reread it. Track your favorite parts of the passage, from use of language, to concept, to character development. Whatever aspect of the work feels most interesting to you, pinpoint that and extract it. Use the rest of your prompt time to continue to develop and expand this piece in whatever way you see fit.

# Writing Sample

**1-MINUTE PROMPT:** Quick! Set the timer and go! Don't think too much; just let the words tumble out. If the writing seems disjointed or even nonsensical, you're on the right track. Save what you wrote to do the next prompt when ready.

### SAMPLE:

I am here, hidden from view. I can see you with her. You racing ahead, she falling behind. And then you turn to look, and she pedals faster. It's game on. What a beautiful sight on a Sunday night. I'm dreaming of times gone by with my dad boating on the bay, the way it seemed like we were flying just above the water.

**5-MINUTE PROMPT:** Grab the writing you did from the previous prompt. Extract any interesting two- and three-word pairings. Keeping them in their original order, add text between and around these snippets to create a narrative.

**SAMPLE:**

I am here, but you aren't. If I squint I can see you across the way. I can see you racing ahead. I can see you falling behind. I worry you're going to crash when you turn to look as a girl, maybe only five years old, darts out from a nearby driveway. She follows, mimicking your rhythm. You pedal. She pedals. You move together along the sidewalk, each trying to outdo the other. Game on. I watch until you're both out of sight. My heart aches at your absence. I stare at the place you just were, thinking of times gone by. I wonder if I'm dreaming. There's a memory poking at me. Something we did once. What was it? It was windy, I know that. And cold. How old were we? I don't know, but I'm pretty sure—yes, I'm almost positive—we were flying.

# What's Going On in There?

## 1-MINUTE PROMPT:

Ahh, it's a lovely summer evening for a stroll. As you pass by the neighbor's house you notice a light on in the basement and a strange noise coming from within. You stop to listen. What do you imagine they're doing in there?

## 5-MINUTE PROMPT:

You're getting ready for bed one night when you glance out the window to see a squad of police cars parked in front of your neighbor's home. The next afternoon their space is totally empty. What might have happened?

# 10-MINUTE PROMPT:

The abandoned building next to where you work is starting to show signs of life, despite the fact you've never seen anyone coming or going. As you're leaving work one day you notice something particularly odd about the space next door. What is it?

# 20-MINUTE PROMPT:

You're hard at work on the construction site when, suddenly, everything comes to a halt. A bulldozer has uncovered something very concerning. The Big Boss arrives, along with a team of people wearing hazmat suits, and all hell breaks loose. Write about what happens next.

# The Whole Truth, Sorta

## 1-MINUTE PROMPT:

A court reporter is typing notes during a criminal case against a mafia kingpin. Create an excerpt from their transcripts.

## 5-MINUTE PROMPT:

A judge presiding over a criminal case against a mafia don orders a bailiff to throw a man out of the courtroom. Start the scene with the man's outburst and end it when the doors close on him.

# 10-MINUTE PROMPT:

A witness who's being cross-examined looks really nervous during the trial of a mob boss. Write a courtroom scene about the witness's testimony and use flashbacks to show previous involvement between the witness and the mob boss.

# 20-MINUTE PROMPT:

After an exhaustive investigation police are finally able to gather enough evidence to arrest a well-known leader of an organized crime family. Imagine you're an investigative journalist who's able to take a sneak peek at some of the documents inside this criminal's case file. There's photographic evidence, witness statements, surveillance video, and more. How strong is this case? Is the evidence solid or not? Write your first-person impressions in the style of questions and thoughts jotted down in a reporter's notebook.

# Vaguely Presidential

## 1-MINUTE PROMPT:

The votes are in and, yup, you've been chosen to be president of your neighborhood association. What's the first thing you'd like to address?

## 5-MINUTE PROMPT:

What are you an absolute fanatic about? Imagine you're now president of the fan club. What would you like to do as president? What's the best way you can honor that to which you're devoted?

# 10-MINUTE PROMPT:

It was a tight election race, but you did it. Congrats, you're president of the galaxy! Your first task is to draft a declaration to be read and discussed at the next intergalactic council meeting. What will you include in the document?

# 20-MINUTE PROMPT:

It's a tough job, but someone's got to do it. Congrats, Prez, you're now in charge of the nation. It's time to get to work on the inaugural address. First decide what kind of tone you want to set—whether it's idealistic, persuasive, reassuring, or otherwise—then touch on the biggest issues you believe this country is facing. End your address with a rallying cry intended to unite the citizens.

# Living Earth

## 1-MINUTE PROMPT:

*Shhh, you hear that?* Lean your ear down to the ground. There's a wee insect that would like to share something with you. What does it have to say?

## 5-MINUTE PROMPT:

From the prairies to the savannas, grasses of all kinds cover the planet. Imagine if you could understand the language that grass speaks. What kind of stories would it be able to tell? Write a prose poem or poetic essay about grass as a living witness to all of life on Earth.

# 10-MINUTE PROMPT:

Nearly three-quarters of the earth is covered by water, and more than half of our own bodies is made of the stuff. (I know, mind-blowing, right?) What if we could go into a sort of dream state and communicate with water? Imagine the stories it could tell about shipwrecks, ocean creatures, rainy days, or what it's like to exist inside of our bodies. Pretend water is an old man who's pulled up a chair and is eager to tell you a tale. Transcribe it.

# 20-MINUTE PROMPT:

There are more than seven billion people on planet Earth, each one of them ripe with experiences and stories. Imagine you've been tasked with a very special project for NASA—to collect one story from ten everyday people around the world. The goal is to best represent what it's like to be a human on Earth. Once finished, the stories will be put into a capsule and sent into space with the hope that it reaches intelligent life. What are the profiles of the ten people you choose?

# 1-MINUTE PROMPT:

A person finds a stray receipt on the floor of their car, and one of the items on it really shocks them. Write about it.

# 5-MINUTE PROMPT:

The phone rings. It's the credit card company. An embarrassing purchase has been made on someone's card and the cardholder must explain to the company rep that the purchase wasn't theirs. Write the dialogue from this cringeworthy conversation.

# 10-MINUTE PROMPT:

A man is shopping in the grocery store when a mysterious woman brushes against him. Moments later he notices that she has left something in his shopping cart. What is it, and what does he do next?

# 20-MINUTE PROMPT:

The opening scene of your young adult novel includes a character who wakes up with amnesia. This person has one clue as to who they are and where they've been—a receipt found tucked inside their pants pocket. What purchases are listed there, and how might the receipt help this person retrace their steps and recover their memory?

# 3...2...1

## 1-MINUTE PROMPT:

It's New Year's Eve in Times Square. A couple who have just had an argument stand in silence waiting for the ball to drop. What do they do when midnight arrives? Write about it from a third-person perspective.

## 5-MINUTE PROMPT:

In a darkened movie theater, the film reel counts down, 3...2...1. The movie begins and there's a collective gasp from the audience. What's on the screen? Write about it from the point of view of an omniscient narrator.

# 10-MINUTE PROMPT:

The underdogs have the ball, but they're down by one point with only 3 seconds left on the clock. The player with the basketball needs to make one last shot to secure victory for the team. Write about what happens during the last few seconds of the game as the clock counts down.

# 20-MINUTE PROMPT:

Inside the rocket, the crew is strapped in and ready to go. The atmosphere in Mission Control is focused as flight controllers prepare the launch sequence. The count-down is on. Start with the numbers 3...2...1 and write a story that toggles between a crew member's perspective inside the rocket and that of one of the controllers on the ground.

## 1-MINUTE PROMPT:

You've been given unlimited funds to throw an elaborate dinner. What would the invitation to such a luxe party say?

## 5-MINUTE PROMPT:

An intriguing invite to a dinner party arrives in the mail. When you show up you discover there are ten of you in attendance—you and nine of your clones, each one expressing a different aspect of your personality. What's it like to spend time with yourself in such a way?

# 10-MINUTE PROMPT:

At a high-profile dinner party, you're seated next to a villain. This person could be a fictional character, or a real-life villain such as a serial killer or murderous dictator. What would you most want to know from or about this person? Write your questions and his or her imagined answers.

# 20-MINUTE PROMPT:

It's a question you may have been asked before—if you could put together a dinner party with whomever you like, living or dead, whom would you invite? Imagine you've been given the chance to do that anywhere in the world with any cuisine you'd like. Which famous or unknown people will you assemble for this soirée and what would you like the tone to be—conversational and thoughtful, wild and raucous, or something else entirely? Write a short story that begins in the middle of this event.

# A Captain's Life

## 1-MINUTE PROMPT:

You're team captain now and you have to give your players a pep talk before the big game. What do you say that inspires them?

## 5-MINUTE PROMPT:

In a soon-to-be-released movie, a former Army captain becomes the captain of his daughter's cheerleading squad. Write a plot summary for this film.

# 10-MINUTE PROMPT:

While at a yard sale, you pick up an old handwritten draft of a story that revolves around a character nicknamed Cap'n. As you read, it dawns on you that this might be a lost manuscript of famed author Mark Twain. You take a snapshot of one of the pages and message it to a friend who's a Twain expert to see what she thinks. What does the passage say?

# 20-MINUTE PROMPT:

*Ahoy, Matey!* Being captain of a pirate ship is hard work. You gotta get people to swab the decks, walk the planks, polish the gold, and all sorts of other things. Phew, it's exhausting. Good thing there's a special spa that caters to pirates. Write the spa's pamphlet. Include the names and titles of all their services for maritime marauders.

# Journeys

## 1-MINUTE PROMPT:

What's a place you've always wanted to visit? It could be local, national, out of the country, or even out of this world. Pen a pretend postcard to a friend from that location.

## 5-MINUTE PROMPT:

Think of a place you've traveled to that made a lasting impression. What was it that made it so memorable? Write an ode to this special spot.

# 10-MINUTE PROMPT:

A travel agent has a new client—someone who's visiting Earth for the first time. Create the client's travel itinerary. Be sure to include your choice of notable places around the world and why you consider them must-see spots (even if you've never been there).

# 20-MINUTE PROMPT:

In Homer's epic Greek poem *The Odyssey*, Odysseus crossed paths with many mythological creatures during his travels. What if such a grand journey could take place now? Write a modern-day version of a hero's journey. Perhaps the story revolves around a businessperson's flight to Atlanta for a conference or a housepainter just trying to get through rush hour traffic on her way to work. Whoever the main character is, write the journey so it includes mythological creatures, detours or setbacks, and an ultimate triumph.

# They Doth Protest

## 1-MINUTE PROMPT:

An issue you're particularly passionate about is the focus of an upcoming rally. Create a few clever mottos that could be painted on poster board as signs for the event.

## 5-MINUTE PROMPT:

Think of a divisive issue that you have a strong opinion about. Perhaps it's a widely debated concern that's in the national spotlight, or maybe it's a smaller local issue that's specific to your town or state. Write an op-ed expressing your views on this issue.

# 10-MINUTE PROMPT:

Dissatisfied employees have walked out on the job. After the strike has gone on for a couple of weeks, management brings in a negotiator to try to work out a deal. Unfortunately, the negotiator soon discovers that a vindictive ex-fiancé is among the employees. Write a rom-com scene about their reunion on the picket line.

# 20-MINUTE PROMPT:

There's a feeling of unrest in the air. The possibility of war looms. Unjust policies are put into place causing riots to break out around the country. This is the backdrop of your latest novel. Write an excerpt that begins in the middle of the book.

# Writing Sample

**10-MINUTE PROMPT:** Dissatisfied employees have walked out on the job. After the strike has gone on for a couple of weeks, management brings in a negotiator to try to work out a deal. Unfortunately, the negotiator soon discovers that a vindictive ex-fiancé is among the employees. Write a rom-com scene about their reunion on the picket line.

## SAMPLE:

I can hear them before I see them. Their voices rising above the uneven cacophony of city traffic. A steady chant of "Unfair wages! That's outrageous!" pierces the air. I adjust the buttons on my suit jacket, pull my shoulders back, and breathe in. My first negotiating job and I'm ready to nail this. My confidence wraps around me like a cape. Nothing's getting in my way today. I turn the corner and begin to ping-pong through the throng of striking workers when I hear something that stops me in my tracks. "Oh, this is rich," a familiar voice says. *No. Please don't let it be.* I turn and there he is. Smiling—sarcastically, of course—with those damn perfect teeth. Marcus. My ex-fiancé. "Hello, Marcus," I say, trying to keep my voice even, though the butterflies in my stomach are threatening to fly out of my mouth. *Stay calm, Cal. Maybe he's changed.* Marcus looks me up and down, then spits out an irritated laugh and says, "If you're the negotiator they've brought in, we're screwed. Playing fair certainly isn't your strong suit." He turns back to the picket line and takes up the chant. A sea of people rolls me toward my destination. Despite my shaking hands, I manage to pull open the glass door and duck into the building's foyer. I steal a glance back at the picket line. At Marcus. His dark hair has grown a bit longer and is starting to curl at the ends. The muscles in his perfectly toned neck are stretched taught as he shouts along with his cowork-ers. His neck. The one I used to love to kiss. *Dammit, Cal, focus. You've got to focus.*

# Childhood Fears

## 1-MINUTE PROMPT:

Lots of kids are afraid of the dark—and plenty of adults too. For a change of pace, let's personify darkness and write about what it's afraid of.

## 5-MINUTE PROMPT:

The idea of robbers can captivate and scare a kid. Create the concept of a children's picture book that includes a robber. Is it a well-intentioned robber like Robin Hood, a bad guy robber that needs to learn a lesson, or something else entirely?

# 10-MINUTE PROMPT:

Ever worry about something being under the bed? What if someone pulled up the bed skirt and actually saw something there? Pick a genre—drama, comedy, horror, sci-fi, mystery, romance, and so on—then write a scene in that genre's tone about someone who's discovered something—or someone—under the bed.

# 20-MINUTE PROMPT:

What was your most intense childhood fear? Maybe it was something statistically unlikely like getting kidnapped by a stranger with a van, or maybe it was something unavoidable like embarrassing yourself in front of your peers. Whatever it was, use that fear as character motivation in a scene you might find in a novel with a teenage protagonist.

# Time-Sensitive

## 1-MINUTE PROMPT:

A character is about to be abandoned in a remote location in a foreign country if they can't make it back to the tour bus in time. Write about an obstacle this person must overcome as they race against the clock.

## 5-MINUTE PROMPT:

Your character has been gifted a million bucks, but there's a catch—none of it can be used on himself and it must be spent within two days. How does he decide to spend the money?

# 10-MINUTE PROMPT:

In a vivid dream a dead relative tells you that you have a week to live. To be on the safe side, you decide to spend the next seven days doing only the things you really want to do. Write a journal entry from the perspective of looking back on your week.

# 20-MINUTE PROMPT:

A woman wakes one morning to find a mysterious package on the doorstep. It includes a key, a list of clues, two airline tickets, and a note from a benevolent stranger saying she has 72 hours to locate a life-changing treasure. Write the opening chapter of this adventure story. Include reference to specific clues on the list.

# Strange Object

## 1-MINUTE PROMPT:

A researcher digging through a dusty box of papers in the library's archives finds a strange object inside. Describe the item and make mention of how old it might be.

## 5-MINUTE PROMPT:

Is it a bird...a plane...or a UFO? There's something strange in the night sky. A crowd gathers. Smartphone videos are taken. Theories are discussed. Write a scene that includes snippets of overheard dialogue.

# 10-MINUTE PROMPT:

Police receive a phone call from a homeowner who's fixing his roof. From his higher vantage point he's able to see that there's a large, oddly shaped object in the bottom of a nearby pond. What happens when the police arrive to investigate?

# 20-MINUTE PROMPT:

As the sun sets over the desert, light glints off the surface of a strange object. Write about this wild, quiet place and the strange object that seems incongruous to its surroundings. Consider possible scenarios as to how this object may have ended up there.

# Fallen

## 1-MINUTE PROMPT:

It can happen in an instant. First, you're upright, then suddenly you're flat on the ground. Imagine you've been hired to write a wilderness survival guide. Write some tips on what a person can do if they find themselves in the unfortunate position of having fallen and become injured.

## 5-MINUTE PROMPT:

Two people are falling in love—literally. Pen a short existential tale about a couple who falls in love while endlessly falling through the sky.

# 10-MINUTE PROMPT:

There's a fallen angel in your midst. What sinful thing has this heavenly creature done to lose their wings? What will the fallen angel do now—try to get back into Heaven, or embrace the dark side?

# 20-MINUTE PROMPT:

Someone has cut down an old tree. As this person inspects the tree's growth rings they contemplate their own metaphoric growth rings. What connections could be made between these two different types of growth? What significant life events do these rings mark for both person and tree?

# Once Upon a Time, There Was an Invasion

## 1-MINUTE PROMPT:

You know what it's like when a head cold knocks you sideways. There are the chills, the lethargy, the stuffy head, and all the other yuck of it. But what's the intention of that cold virus? What does it want with you? Write something from the virus's perspective.

## 5-MINUTE PROMPT:

A computer virus is taking over the network of a global financial institution. Tech experts are desperate to stop it before worldwide damage occurs. Write a climactic showdown scene between a child prodigy computer whiz and the virus that's running amok.

# 10-MINUTE PROMPT:

Something insidious has invaded Aaron's life. It's almost imperceptible at first, but as the days roll on things really start to unravel. Somehow, no one else can see what's happening. How can Aaron convince them that the invasion is real so he can save his life?

# 20-MINUTE PROMPT:

Inside the war room there's an assembled group of top-level military officials contemplating an invasion. On the ground, troops are given orders. Planes are fueled. Weapons are loaded. Write about this military operation, whether you're imagining details of an actual historic military invasion or creating a fictitious event. Consider what's happening on the other side of the equation—are there opposing forces readying themselves to fight or is this a sneak attack?

# MEMORY PROMPTS

The prompts in this section are designed to help you recall a variety of life experiences—be they clear, indisputable memories that feel like they happened yesterday or more nebulous and murky ones that seem almost out of reach. You'll be nudged to recall snippets of conversations, or tangible sensations associated with a particular experience, or the accompanying emotions that were stirred up by whatever past memory it is that you're working with. You may be asked to write about these remembrances with specificity, or you may be tasked with using just part of them. In some cases, you'll be re-envisioning your memories entirely. Regardless of the angle at which they're approached, your unique recollections will offer up a concrete platform from which to dive into the creative writing. Many of the prompts in this section will appeal to those who enjoy memoir and personal essays, but—don't fret—equally as many will appeal to fiction enthusiasts too. Ideally, regardless of your predilection, you'll let yourself explore the variety of prompts here and embrace the opportunity to move fluidly between styles and genres along the way.

# Spirits Were Dampened

## 1-MINUTE PROMPT:

People often talk about how rain makes them feel on the inside, but what about the outside? Describe the physical sensations you feel when your skin, hair, and clothes go from dry to wet while standing outside in the rain.

## 5-MINUTE PROMPT:

What does it mean to be soaked to the bone? Remember the thoughts and feelings that arose during a time you got drenched while being out in the rain.

# 10-MINUTE PROMPT:

Rain storms are sensory experiences. Recall how getting caught in the rain once affected all of your senses. What did you see, touch, smell, hear, and taste during that experience? Write a poem about it where each line or stanza begins with a different sense (e.g., "I saw...," "I touched...," "I smelled...," and so on).

# 20-MINUTE PROMPT:

Write the short story of what happened before, during, and after you got caught in the pouring rain once upon a time. Where were you coming from? Where did you end up? How did the rain affect your plans?

# Clothes-Minded

## 1-MINUTE PROMPT:

When it comes down to it, there's a shirt that you like better than all the others. What is it about that shirt that feels so right? Is it the soft texture on your skin, the way you feel while wearing it, the message its slogan conveys, or something else? Take a minute to write a clever and creative clothing catalog product description about this shirt.

## 5-MINUTE PROMPT:

Once upon a time you had a pair of pants. You know the ones I mean? Write an imagined scene where you attend an event while wearing a certain pair of pants that you once owned. What makes you want to wear these pants to this particular event?

# 10-MINUTE PROMPT:

Ugh, remember that time you left a piece of clothing behind? Perhaps you forgot to grab one of your bags before boarding the train, or maybe you vacated someone's apartment a bit too quickly the morning after... *Ahem.* Write a scene where a character leaves the same item of clothing behind. (It doesn't have to be the same place where you left it.) Consider a scenario in which the lost item of clothing has bigger implications than your character might first realize.

# 20-MINUTE PROMPT:

Sometimes clothes are more than just clothes. Maybe it's the apron your grandma wore while baking, the sneakers your nephew sported as he made a full-court shot at the buzzer, or the hand-me-down tux you and your grandfather both got married in. All of these items of clothes have deeper meaning beyond their function. Think of an article of clothing attached to a memory and write about its deeper meaning.

# Bugs, Beasts, and Barbecues

## 1-MINUTE PROMPT:

Wherefore art thou Fido? Recall your first experience with an animal, whether it was a pet or a creature in nature. What lasting impression did it give you?

## 5-MINUTE PROMPT:

Whether it was mosquitoes infiltrating a barbecue or cockroaches invading the kitchen, there was a time when bugs got up in your grill—perhaps even literally. Write a very short story about an entomologic disruption.

# 10-MINUTE PROMPT:

There was an animal that affected your life, the one whose presence changed something within you or around you. Brainstorm some ideas for a children's book about this special beast.

# 20-MINUTE PROMPT:

Write down all the names of pets you can remember, even if they were someone else's. Be sure to remember the lizard, fish, bird, and horse pets too. Imagine that list of names is an attendance sheet at a nontraditional high school. Write a classroom scene with these offbeat characters. How do their names inform their personalities?

# Party Schmarty

## 1-MINUTE PROMPT:

"Party's over, pal" is never something you want to hear. Write about a mishap that caused a party or event to go sideways.

## 5-MINUTE PROMPT:

Remember what happened at that work party? Or should I say, who could forget? Write about it from a point of view that's not your own, whether it's the imagined perspective of another person who was actually there or that of an omniscient narrator.

# 10-MINUTE PROMPT:

Gift giving can be a tricky thing. Recall a gift you received that was inappropriate, misguided, or just totally off the mark. Write about it from the imagined point of view of the gift giver. Try to figure out what mental leaps made this person think the gift was a good idea.

# 20-MINUTE PROMPT:

You know that thing where you're at a party making small talk and you say something that you immediately wish you could take back? Yeah, that. (Insert cringing here.) Think of a time when you blurted something out that you wish you hadn't said. Use that as a jumping-off point for a freestyle, stream-of-consciousness dialogue scene between two characters.

# Angels in Our Midst

## 1-MINUTE PROMPT:

Ever had a stranger hook you up with a favor? Using one- and two-word sentences only, write a short story about a time a stranger did you a solid.

## 5-MINUTE PROMPT:

Every now and again our lives are made better by strangers who have no idea they've helped us, like someone who accidentally dropped a twenty-dollar bill that you stumbled upon at just the right moment. Using a third-person perspective, write about a time when a stranger or group of strangers helped you without even knowing it.

# 10-MINUTE PROMPT:

Phew, you showed up in the nick of time! Somewhere along the way you happened upon a person in need of assistance and extended a helping hand. Using details from that encounter, write a scene from a novel where fate brings two characters together.

# 20-MINUTE PROMPT:

Sometimes a stranger goes above and beyond for us then seems to vanish. We're left wondering, *Whoa, did that really just happen*? Remember a time when you found yourself in a real pinch and an "earth angel" arrived to save you. Start with the facts as you recall them, then continue with a fictional account of what the stranger did after he or she left you.

# Writing Sample

**1-MINUTE PROMPT:** Ever had a stranger hook you up with a favor? Using one- and two-word sentences only, write a short story about a time a stranger did you a solid.

## SAMPLE:

Mountain road. Flat tire. Lug wrench. Struggle, strain. Won't budge. Car stops. Boots approaching. Strong hands. Lefty-loosey. Clank, clatter. Tire off. Spare on. Righty-tighty. Driving away.

# Food Is Love

## 1-MINUTE PROMPT:

What's your all-time desert island food? Write the opening lines of a stand-up comedy monologue that mentions this food.

## 5-MINUTE PROMPT:

A food blogger wants to include you in a post about childhood cooking experiences. Write a quote for her that recalls an experience when someone taught you to cook or bake something.

# 10-MINUTE PROMPT:

Think of a special meal that you once ate. Maybe it was the first solid food you gobbled up after a long illness, or maybe it was something you shared with a love interest on a first date. Write a short essay about nostalgia in the context of this meal.

# 20-MINUTE PROMPT:

Cast your mind back to a meal that was unforgettable to your palate—the bliss-inducing Baja-style fish tacos, or the creamiest vegan mac-n-cheese, or the to-die-for chicken and waffles with real maple syrup...you get the picture. Whatever it was, do some writing about it from the point of view of a death row inmate requesting it as his last meal.

# Scalpel, Please

## 1-MINUTE PROMPT:

What's that old saying…"Surgery happens"? Something like that. (Shrug.) Pen a tiny poem about one thing you remember about a surgery that took place. If you didn't have an operation, maybe someone you know did—even if that someone was just a character on a favorite TV show.

## 5-MINUTE PROMPT:

Scalpels. Hospital beds. IV drips. Remember that time someone had an operation? Take a minute to jot down what you can remember about the situation, then use your notes to create the inner monologue of a character awaiting surgery.

# 10-MINUTE PROMPT:

It's likely you or someone you love has been "under the knife," if only for something undramatic like, say, a wisdom tooth extraction. See if you can recall how you or others felt about a surgery that took place. Whether it was relief, terror, resistance, or something else, write about the emotional aspects of the surgery from the point of view of those involved.

# 20-MINUTE PROMPT:

The prospect of surgery can be a scary one. But what if it was set to music and given some catchy lyrics? Imagine a surgery that you or someone you know had to undergo. Rewrite the story of that procedure as a musical number in a Broadway hit.

# Heart = Broken

## 1-MINUTE PROMPT:

Heartbreak is a universal experience. Think of a time when your heart felt shattered. Imagine the story of your heartbreak is going to premiere in living color on the Hallmark Channel. Brainstorm a list of movie titles that aptly describe what happened.

## 5-MINUTE PROMPT:

People handle breakups in all kinds of ways, from endless ranting and raving, to lying around depressed. What about you—how did you cope after a big breakup? Write your younger self a letter offering thoughts and advice on how to deal with the post-breakup blues.

# 10-MINUTE PROMPT:

Let's turn the tables. Remember a time when you experienced unrequited love. Rewrite that story of heartbreak where, this time, you are the one who isn't interested in the other person. Will you let the besotted one down easy or flip your hair and sashay away?

# 20-MINUTE PROMPT:

Heartbreak isn't reserved for romantic relationships. Kids, parents, coworkers, pets, and friends cause pangs in our tickers too. Do some freewriting about a memory where your heart got broken in a nonromantic situation—then throw in an element of magical realism to the mix and see where it leads you.

# Burning Desire

## 1-MINUTE PROMPT:

We all have desires. What are yours? Create a piece where every sentence starts with the words "I want."

## 5-MINUTE PROMPT:

Something you deeply want is just out of reach—a relationship, a job, a new home, better health. An unlikely assassin has this very same desire. How does this desire inform what the assassin does for a living?

# 10-MINUTE PROMPT:

There was a time when you wanted something, but you didn't get it—and that ended up being a good thing. Mention this in an excerpt from a keynote address you could give at a college graduation.

# 20-MINUTE PROMPT:

Then there was a time you got something you really wanted, and, boy, was that a problem. Do some freestyle writing about the unintended results, then take that writing and craft some lines of a song about it.

# The Accident

## 1-MINUTE PROMPT:

Remember when someone broke something of yours. What was it? How did you feel about it?

## 5-MINUTE PROMPT:

Remember the car accident (one that happened or almost happened) that you still think of and shudder? Write a scene from a screenplay about it that ends just before the moment of impact.

# 10-MINUTE PROMPT:

Whether you tripped and fell down a flight of stairs or burned yourself while cooking, it's likely you've had accidents in your life. Make a list of as many as you can remember, then turn the list into case notes that you might find in a doctor's file.

# 20-MINUTE PROMPT:

Can you keep a reader on the edge of their seat? Write about an accident you remember happening to you or someone else in the style of a thriller novel. Use a combination of short one-word sentences and longer descriptive sentences. Stay conscious of building tension as you lead up to the accident.

# One Nation

## 1-MINUTE PROMPT:

Emotional experiences leave an imprint on your memory. Where were you and what were you doing when you heard that a beloved national figure died?

## 5-MINUTE PROMPT:

Remember a time when you voted in a national election. How did it feel to cast your vote? Write your experience with the ballot box from the perspective of a twelve-year-old kid who's just finished voting for president of his or her middle school class.

# 10-MINUTE PROMPT:

Whether it was the Olympics, the World Cup, the Super Bowl, or the World Series, you once watched a sporting event that the whole country was watching too. Did you feel a sense of national pride, of camaraderie, or not? Did you experience a sense of victory, or one of crushing defeat?

# 20-MINUTE PROMPT:

An event happened that seemed to bring everyone together. Depending on your age that could be JFK's assassination or Harry and Meghan's royal wedding. Where were you and what were you doing when an event like this happened? Create an opinion piece about it for a prominent news outlet. Explore the relevance of this event in light of today's world.

# AGGHHH!

## 1-MINUTE PROMPT:

Panic is a terrible feeling. Using a memory of a time that you panicked, craft the slogan for a bus advertisement aiming to calm people found in that exact scenario.

## 5-MINUTE PROMPT:

Think of a time you panicked. What if, unbeknownst to you, behavioral scientists were studying you? What did your panic look like from the outside? Write up an observation report about your panicky behavior from the point of view of the scientists.

# 10-MINUTE PROMPT:

After a bout of panic, there's a period of relief. Write about what it's like to experience that relief in your heart, mind, body, and soul after something utterly freaks you out. How does everything return to normal again?

# 20-MINUTE PROMPT:

Think of a time when you panicked in the presence of another person. Write out this scene as though it takes place in a different historical time period. (Choose a decade that's at least fifty years in the past.) What about that historic time period would change the details of your panicky situation?

# Nevertheless, She Persisted

 ## 1-MINUTE PROMPT:

Think of a time when someone you know wanted to quit. What would you write in a note to encourage that person to keep going?

 ## 5-MINUTE PROMPT:

Remember when you wanted to throw in the towel, but you didn't? How did that situation resolve? Write an ending to a story where the protagonist pushes through in the same way that you did.

# 10-MINUTE PROMPT:

Recall a woman (or girl) from history who persisted against the odds and brought something special to the world. It could be someone well known, or it could be someone important to you personally such as a familial ancestor. Write about an obstacle this person was up against and what her persistence means to you.

# 20-MINUTE PROMPT:

Persistence isn't always a good thing. Think of someone you know who persisted when, truth be told, they should've packed it in a lot sooner. Using the details of your friend or acquaintance's experience, write a short cautionary tale about knowing when to quit.

# Into the Medicine Cabinet

## 1-MINUTE PROMPT:

Aches, pains, and maybe sprains? Think of a kind of medicine you once used for an ailment. Write a short rhyme about it.

## 5-MINUTE PROMPT:

You were sick. You took medicine. Write the text of a TV script for a pharmaceutical ad about this medicine you took. Include some outlandish and nonsensical side effects.

# 10-MINUTE PROMPT:

Have you ever experienced the cathartic effect of journaling, or the medicinal benefit of a home-cooked meal when you were under the weather? Think of your favorite non-pharmaceutical forms of medicine and write about them.

# 20-MINUTE PROMPT:

Studies show that nature can have medicinal effects on the body, mind, and spirit. Recall a healing experience you had with nature, whether it was the awe of standing beneath a towering redwood tree, the encouragement of seeing a flower grow up through a sidewalk crack, or the happiness of snuggling with a puppy. Mention your recollection of this "natural medicine" experience in an origin story about an ecological superhero(ine). Of course, don't forget to note your hero's superpower and how it helps the planet.

# Fightin' Words

## 1-MINUTE PROMPT:

RAAAWWWWR! Have you ever had an argument or disagreement with someone that got you so upset you didn't feel like yourself? Perhaps it was your alter ego peeking through, sort of like The Incredible Hulk, you know? Come up with the name and stats of an alter ego who could emerge when you get fired up.

## 5-MINUTE PROMPT:

Sometimes you say the right thing, and sometimes you don't. Think of a heat-of-the-moment comment that you or someone else once said during an argument. Use that line to open a story about a couple who are trapped, be it physically or emotionally.

# 10-MINUTE PROMPT:

Remember when you got snippy with someone and regretted it later? (Ugh. Hate that.) Re-envision that situation as a comedy skit where the snippy comment kicks off an absurd tête-à-tête between two people.

# 20-MINUTE PROMPT:

You know those arguments that never quite resolve, the ones where, even though people apologized, there's still some residual hard feelings kicking around? Think of a conflict in your life that isn't fully resolved. Write about it in the form of an advice column that includes a reader's letter and the columnist's advice.

# Writing Sample

**1-MINUTE PROMPT:** RAAAWWWWR! Have you ever had an argument or disagreement with someone that got you so upset you didn't feel like yourself? Perhaps it was your alter ego peeking through, sort of like The Incredible Hulk, you know? Come up with the name and stats of an alter ego who could emerge when you get fired up.

**SAMPLE:**

Alter Ego: Fauna Firestarter. Age: seventy-five human years. Diminutive in size, but majestic in stature. This weathered crone, with hair of flames and nerves of steel, can incinerate her enemies with a single glance.

# Reimagined and It Feels So Good

## 1-MINUTE PROMPT:

Congrats! You won a Webby Award for "excellence on the Internet." Remember something you once did online (even if it's as simple as composing a particularly eloquent email), and pretend you're being honored for that. Turns out that Webby acceptance speeches are notoriously short at five words a pop. What will your five words be?

## 5-MINUTE PROMPT:

What details do you know about your own birth? Take whatever they are and use them in a story about a child's arrival from the location of a zero-gravity rocket ship.

# 10-MINUTE PROMPT:

Let's be real: words hurt just as much as sticks and stones—sometimes even more. Think of a letter, email, text, or verbal takedown you once received that gutted you. Imagine what you wish the person addressing you would've said instead. How would that re-envisioning make what came next different?

# 20-MINUTE PROMPT:

Abracadabra! Imagine you're given the chance to rewrite one event from history. What would you change if you had the chance? How would the world be different with your revisions?

# It Happens Periodically

## 1-MINUTE PROMPT:

Remember learning about the periodic table as a kid? Let's revisit it. What's an experience you've had that involves the element of calcium (Ca)? It could be anything from how you chipped a tooth to the first time you ate ice cream.

## 5-MINUTE PROMPT:

Chlorine (Cl) is an element most known for keeping swimming pools nice and blue. Think of a time you took a dip. Write a poem about the experience using rich visual imagery. Consider the colors, shapes, sizes, and textures of the experience.

# 10-MINUTE PROMPT:

Without this element there would be no balloon animals! Yup, I'm talking about helium (He). Think of an event you attended that used balloons in some way. Using that event as a backdrop, write a scene from a mystery novel. Be sure to include a loud *pop*.

# 20-MINUTE PROMPT:

Sodium (Na) is one of two elements that make up salt, which can be found in our bodies, our oceans, our meals, and sometimes—if we've had a long day—our bathwater. Think of an experience where salt played a crucial factor. Write an essay titled "Salted" for a literary journal.

# Nice and Not-So-Nice Advice

## 1-MINUTE PROMPT:

"Here lies Lianne. She always got enough sleep." Parental types are infamous for doling out advice, not all of which should be rigidly heeded. Think of some advice a parent or older person once gave you and use it to craft an epitaph.

## 5-MINUTE PROMPT:

Ever receive some questionable advice about dating? Maybe it was about playing hard to get. Maybe it was convincing you to make a grand gesture. Whatever it was, write about it in a scene at a train station where a character takes the advice you got and has some unexpected results.

# 10-MINUTE PROMPT:

Maybe you don't realize it, but you dole out advice from time to time. Maybe it's tips about folding laundry, or maybe it's about finding a good mechanic. Think of the most recent advice you gave to someone then use it in an excerpt from a romantic comedy where the main character is a life coach.

# 20-MINUTE PROMPT:

Whether it was a performance review or a sidebar from your boss, you once were given some advice at work. Was it helpful? Enraging? Both? Use the advice to write dialogue for a stage play about an employee. Create at least two changes of scenery.

# Warm and Fuzzy?

 ## 1-MINUTE PROMPT:

Awkward hugs are the worst. Think of a cringe-inducing squeeze you'd rather not have experienced and write about it. Painful as it might be to recall, don't spare the details.

 ## 5-MINUTE PROMPT:

Did you ever envelop someone with a hug or become enveloped in a hug that you never wanted to end? Write your recollections of one of those deeply satisfying hugs, but...make one of you a ghost in this scenario. How would that supernatural switcheroo change the experience of this hug, not only just physically but metaphysically too?

# 10-MINUTE PROMPT:

What about a group hug? Perhaps it was your fantasy football bros or a bunch of cousins at a family reunion, but somewhere down the line you shared a celebratory group hug. Write a scene from a dystopian novel that begins with a group hug like the one you recall.

# 20-MINUTE PROMPT:

Generally speaking, what types of hugs do you prefer—long, deep hugs, or short ones with little physical contact? Maybe you think the best hug is no hug at all? Using your own personal experience of a lifetime of hugging—or not—put together a how-to guide on hugging people.

# Nightscape

## 1-MINUTE PROMPT:

Think of a time you stayed up all night. Describe your memory of the sky's transition from dark to light during sunrise.

## 5-MINUTE PROMPT:

Which do you prefer, the glow of the streetlights or the glow of the Milky Way? Imagine that night, with all of its natural and man-made ambience, has its own *Yelp* page. Give night a review that makes mention of a memory of something that happened after the sun went down.

# 10-MINUTE PROMPT:

Remember a time you enjoyed an evening outside, whether it was camping in the woods or strolling a carnival while noshing on some cotton candy. Write about your experience as though it's an excerpt from the middle of a novel. Let the plot and characters take you where they will, even if it veers from your memory.

# 20-MINUTE PROMPT:

Brainstorm a list of sights and sounds that you've experienced at night, from fireworks to dance parties to insomnia. Use the items on the list to make up a supernatural manual or dictionary that outlines the favorite activities of creatures of the night, such as ghosts, demons, werewolves, vampires, and other monsters.

# Best. Feeling. Ever.

## 1-MINUTE PROMPT:

What's one thing that made you happy this week? Brainstorm a list of hyperbolic self-help book titles about it.

## 5-MINUTE PROMPT:

It felt like you'd never get there, but then—Kapow!—all your hard work paid off. Write a letter to someone about an experience that made you feel accomplished. Frame it in a before/after scenario to highlight your successful trajectory.

# 10-MINUTE PROMPT:

No one likes to hear the phrase "I told you so," even though we sometimes really, really want to say it. Think of a time when you felt vindicated. Then, using details from that experience, write the closing lines or paragraphs from a chapter in your latest novel.

# 20-MINUTE PROMPT:

There's a reason that the word *pride* is often coupled with the word *bursting*. It fills us up. When have you felt a sense of overwhelming pride? Write the text for a nightly anchor's news story about your proud moment. Start with something along the lines of: "An area resident is feeling an overwhelming sense of pride today." Be sure to throw in a fictitious interview quote from a witness or bystander.

# Worst. Feeling. Ever.

## 1-MINUTE PROMPT:

*Ew. Yuck. Blech.* Disgust makes your skin crawl, doesn't it? Compose a 140-character (or less) social media post about something you can recall that made you feel disgusted.

## 5-MINUTE PROMPT:

Is there anything in the world that makes us want to get a fake passport and shed our identities more than a mortifying experience? If you can stomach it, pull up a memory related to feelings of embarrassment or humiliation. Use one-, two-, and three-word sentences to write about this cringe-inducing experience.

# 10-MINUTE PROMPT:

Have you ever trembled with rage? Plot out a swash-buckling adventure story where the main character's fury (based on your own memory of fury) is a catalyst to the action. What is the character's main goal? Whom will this character challenge to a duel along the way?

# 20-MINUTE PROMPT:

Whether it was contending with a family member who let you down, grappling with the aftermath of a goal you didn't reach, or being witness to someone else's bad behavior, something once made you feel pretty disappointed. Use the memory of the related feelings as inspiration for a personal essay.

# Spooked Out

## 1-MINUTE PROMPT:

Ever get a weird phone call or text message that, even to this day, creeps you out when you think of it? Write about the call or message and how you felt receiving it.

## 5-MINUTE PROMPT:

Someone walking behind you in the dark on an empty street. A window you don't remember leaving open. A stranger who sits uncomfortably close to you on an otherwise empty bus. Whatever happened, it made you feel unsettled. Write about it in the form of an opening paragraph of a dark comedy novel.

# 10-MINUTE PROMPT:

Have you ever experienced something that can't be explained? Did it make you feel disturbed or reassured? Create a pitch for a TV pilot that's based on this inexplicable happening.

# 20-MINUTE PROMPT:

Once upon a time, you or someone you know saw a ghost. Use the memory of that experience—even if it was a secondhand retelling—to write a persuasive essay about the existence or nonexistence of the supernatural.

# To Eat, Perchance to Savor

## 1-MINUTE PROMPT:

What's the last thing you drank? Write the lines of dialogue that a person rescued from the desert might say after taking a large gulp of whatever your most recent beverage was.

## 5-MINUTE PROMPT:

Food, glorious food! What's the most delicious and/or satisfying thing that you've eaten in the past 24 hours? Use it as inspiration to craft some text for a children's early reader book.

# 10-MINUTE PROMPT:

Everyone has a signature dish. Maybe yours is as straight-forward as a tuna casserole or maybe it's as complicated as a three-cheese lobster risotto garnished with chives and pea shoots. Think of a time when you made your signature dish. Use the experience to write a quietly dra-matic scene with two characters who have reunited after a long period of estrangement.

# 20-MINUTE PROMPT:

Blech! As much as it pains you, cast your mind back to a time you unwittingly ate or drank something that tasted absolutely wretched. Write of your experience in the style of a podcast episode or radio news story. Is there a nar-rator? What interviews would be included? Consider that there might be a larger cultural or societal commentary of your distasteful food experience.

# Memory Loss

## 1-MINUTE PROMPT:

Remember a time when you forgot to hit Save and lost something you were working on. What was it and why did it matter? Write a limerick that starts with a line such as: "There once was an unsaved draft."

## 5-MINUTE PROMPT:

*Oopsie.* Remember when you didn't call someone back and there were repercussions? Make mention of your experience in a summary that could go on the back of a young adult novel. Explain how dropping the ball on the phone call set off a chain of events in this teen tale.

# 10-MINUTE PROMPT:

Once upon a time you forgot to do one small thing and you felt mortified about it. Whether it was logging out of an embarrassing website, forgetting to tuck away your journal before your mom came over, or accidentally leaving the blinds open while you were in the shower, think of an experience of forgetfulness that led to embarrassment and write about it. Use a third-person perspective and change some details if that makes it easier to stomach the memory.

# 20-MINUTE PROMPT:

You said you'd do it, but then you forgot. That got you into trouble. Of course that's only because you can't tell anyone you're involved with international espionage. Write the story of an imagined mission that caused you to forget a very real obligation. Be sure to throw a cool spy gadget or two into the mix.

# Seasons and Reasons

## 1-MINUTE PROMPT:

What do you love the most about the winter season? What do you hate about it? Write a short compare/contrast piece about these winter opposites.

## 5-MINUTE PROMPT:

Recall a summer day that you really enjoyed. Whether it was hanging out on a roof watching fireworks over the city skyline, kicking it with friends in the park, or soaking up the sun on a picturesque beach, write about what you did on this summer day. Craft it as a diary entry from the point of view of a famous historical character.

# 10-MINUTE PROMPT:

What are your favorite spring activities? Write a faux almanac entry predicting the weather in your area for next spring. Include specific mentions of seasonal things you like to do and how the weather might affect them.

# 20-MINUTE PROMPT:

Fall brings pumpkin spice and everything nice. Or does it? Remember a less-than-pleasant experience that happened during the fall, whether it was failing a school entrance exam or hosting a Halloween party that went awry. Mention the incident in a college admissions essay you compose about the perils of the fall season.

# Writing Sample

**5-MINUTE PROMPT:** Recall a summer day that you really enjoyed. Whether it was hanging out on a roof watching fireworks over the city skyline, kicking it with friends in the park, or soaking up the sun on a picturesque beach, write about what you did on this summer day. Craft it as a diary entry from the point of view of a famous historical character.

**SAMPLE:**

The limbo stick was a cinch at first, but as it progressively got lowered I found myself unable to bend the way I could in my youth. Nonetheless, my seafaring comrades fell by the wayside as the game went on and, the next thing you know, I'd won a bottle of Caribbean rum. I say, it surprised me as much as anyone else. For the rest of the night folks were slapping me on the back. It was all, "Good job, Ben," and "How'd you get so flexible, B-Frank?" These old bones aren't out of commission yet, it seems. Afterwards, I found myself on the top deck looking up at the sky. I began to think, what if I had done the kite experiment from the deck of a boat instead of in a field? Surely the results would've been the same. The ocean is a powerful place to be during a lightning storm. My mind wandered until a rousing chorus of "99 Bottles of Beer on the Wall" snapped me out of my reverie. I hurried to join them before the buzz wore off.

# Rites (and Wrongs) of Passage

## 1-MINUTE PROMPT:

Remember your very first date? Pretend you're being questioned by police about it. Write a short witness statement about something seemingly benign that occurred on your date.

## 5-MINUTE PROMPT:

First days of school are memorable, but not always in the best way. Sometimes not-so-pleasant things happen, like peeing your pants in kindergarten, or being called out by your professor in a lecture hall full of hundreds of your peers, or overhearing kids making fun of the substitute teacher who happened to be, um, you. Do some freestyle writing about an unfortunate experience on the first day of school.

# 10-MINUTE PROMPT:

Think of a maiden voyage you took on a set of wheels—whether it was a skateboard, a tricycle, a car, or some other method of transport. Recall the feeling of nervous excitement as you first started to roll. Write a memoir excerpt about it.

# 20-MINUTE PROMPT:

Graduation days can be bittersweet occasions. Sometimes there's uncertainty about the future, or sadness about leaving friends behind. Remember something that triggered a mixture of sadness and happiness in you on a day that you or someone else graduated. Create a character study based on the real-life graduate, then write a passage from a novel in which details of the graduation—and your accompanying emotions—are featured.

# Unlikely Teachers

## 1-MINUTE PROMPT:

Somewhere along the line life treated you badly. Despite the fact that the situation was entirely unfair, you learned a tough lesson that was ultimately very valuable. Sum up this hard-earned lesson in the style of a motivational quote.

## 5-MINUTE PROMPT:

Every now and again strangers cross our paths who wind up educating us about something, whether it's how to pump gas or how to heal from a broken heart. Write about a stranger who spontaneously, and perhaps unknowingly, educated you.

# 10-MINUTE PROMPT:

Not all teachers are alike. Some of them are—let's face it—duds. Think of a teacher, professor, or mentor who was a dud but ended up affecting your life in a positive way regardless. Was this positive outcome because of this person or in spite of them?

# 20-MINUTE PROMPT:

One could argue that anything you learn from is a teacher. By that loose definition, a spider that meticulously rebuilds its web no matter how many times it gets destroyed can teach you about resilience. Along the way you've likely had a bunch of nonhuman and/or fictional teachers. Think of one that inspired you to grow and evolve. Create a biography of whoever—or whatever—this teacher is.

# Rejected, Reviewed, Rewritten, Rethunk

## 1-MINUTE PROMPT:

Ever have an idea that wouldn't stop nagging you? Sometimes ideas pester us even when we know they're fundamentally bad. Think of a questionable idea that's been rattling around in your noggin and compose a short rejection letter to it.

## 5-MINUTE PROMPT:

Some businesses are out of this world. Think of one that you've visited recently, whether it's the dry cleaner or the convenience store, and write the inner monologue of a Greek god or goddess who's come down from Mount Olympus to check this place out.

# 10-MINUTE PROMPT:

Ever read a book that you felt kind of *meh* about? Perhaps you even said to yourself, *I could write something better than this*. Well, here's your chance to make the case. Craft a short essay that details what you would change about the story. Would you rewrite the plot? Would you alter anything about the characters or setting?

# 20-MINUTE PROMPT:

Write a critical analysis of a recent TV episode you watched, taking into account the visuals, dialogue, and devices that were used to convey the show's message or theme. What worked, and what didn't? Lay out a case for whether the show's creator achieved what he or she appeared to be intending to achieve.

# Muse-ical

# 1-MINUTE PROMPT:

Music connects us to people and places in a very particular way. What pop song evokes a certain person or place for you? Take a lyric from that song and imagine it's a line of dialogue spoken by one character to another. What would the second character say in response to this line?

# 5-MINUTE PROMPT:

Children's songs are intended to be memorable, which makes them relentless earworms. Think of a classic nursery rhyme and imagine you've been tasked with adapting the lyrics from it into an advertising jingle for a hotel chain or car rental agency.

# 10-MINUTE PROMPT:

People sometimes get so overcome with emotion that they burst into song. Maybe it was you singing in the shower, or maybe it was a drunken bachelorette party on the subway that got everyone warbling. Whatever the situation may have been, use your real-life remembrance of an impromptu sing-along to create an article written from a first-person perspective.

# 20-MINUTE PROMPT:

Did you ever find yourself at a friend's house while his band practices for their next gig or accidentally collide with a high school marching band as they stroll by? Remember an experience where you happened upon something musical. Take the details of that event and write a scene where the musician or musicians are playing a wedding. Is the music a great fit or a disastrous choice? Set the tone of the scene with the music, then keep writing to see what happens next.

# What a Tool

## 1-MINUTE PROMPT:

Humans have had tools for nearly three million years, but it's only in the last couple hundred that we've designed them for personal hygiene. Think of the tools you use to keep yourself groomed: the toothbrush, the hair comb, the washcloth, and more. Pick one of these tools and describe the experience of using it.

## 5-MINUTE PROMPT:

Think of a kitchen tool that you have a particular affinity for, whether it's a special coffee mug or a favorite frying pan. Use this tool in a scene that takes place in a kitchen. Write it from the point of view of a baby watching a parent.

# 10-MINUTE PROMPT:

We have lots of tools for communication. Think of one that you use regularly, such as a computer or smartphone, and pair it with a communication tool you've never used, such as skywriting or Morse code. Create a scene from a silent film script where two characters have a back-and-forth conversation using these tools.

# 20-MINUTE PROMPT:

What's a tool that you rely on that you wish you didn't have to? Perhaps it's something like jumper cables for your old truck or reading glasses for diminishing eyesight. Using aspects of your own interactions with this tool, see if you can symbolically connect its functionality to a larger aspect of your life in a memoir excerpt.

# Zombie Mode

## 1-MINUTE PROMPT:

Have you ever been so tired that your tiredness was tired? Think of an occasion where you were so tired that you felt like the living dead. Write about the physical experience of deep exhaustion. Where in your body did you feel it?

## 5-MINUTE PROMPT:

Once upon a time there was a project you thought was dead, but—lo and behold!—it came back to life. Imagine that this revived project played an instrumental part in national security. Write about it from the point of view of an agent with the National Security Agency (NSA).

# 10-MINUTE PROMPT:

You know that thing where you're just getting over your ex, and then they start coming around again? Recall a time when a romance you thought was dead wasn't. Dramatize your experience and write it as a climactic scene in a timeless romance story.

# 20-MINUTE PROMPT:

When a beloved movie, book, TV, or stage character dies we sometimes feel actual sadness, even though we know we're dealing with a fictitious person. What character's death affected you? Imagine that character coming back—as a zombie. What now?

# Fantastic Fandom

## 1-MINUTE PROMPT:

*A Tree Grows in Terabithia*? Take the plotlines of two favorite books and mash them up so you can create a one-sentence plot summary about this literary hybrid.

## 5-MINUTE PROMPT:

If you could spend a day with a favorite fictional character, who would it be and where would you go? Taking into consideration your character's personality, likes and dislikes, and more, write about a special day when you played host to this unlikely visitor.

# 10-MINUTE PROMPT:

What if you could re-envision a different ending to a favorite film? Perhaps it's an animated classic that you watched over and over as a kid, or maybe it's a subtitled foreign film that makes you feel transported. Jot down your remembrances of the movie's ending, then rewrite it anew.

# 20-MINUTE PROMPT:

What's your all-time, hands-down favorite TV show? Take a piece of paper and rip or cut it into pieces. Write down some locations, one on each of the pieces. (Locations may be as varied as your neighborhood butcher shop or the Great Pyramid of Giza.) Fold up the pieces, shuffle them around, then choose one. Write some fan fiction of your favorite show that takes place at the location you've picked. Consider how the location creates new opportunities for the characters within their individual storylines or subplots.

# INDEX